The Clown King
Popular Entertainment 1840-1860

Also by Gareth H. H. Davies

The Fall of Yarmouth Suspension Bridge:
A Norfolk Disaster

The Clown King
Popular Entertainment 1840-1860

GARETH H. H. DAVIES

companion website
www.theclownking.com

To Olwen

What is the difference between Mr Dowling the fowl merchant and Clown
Nelson?
The one draws geese, the other is drawn by geese.

Conundrum entered in a competition at Bell's American Circus, while performing
at Howard Street, Belfast March 1855.

Contents

Acknowledgements

This book started as an unanswered conundrum when writing my previous volume on the fall of Yarmouth Suspension Bridge (see chapter 4). Those who hear me speak on the disaster often ask what happened to the unfortunate clown who was the catalyst for that dreadful afternoon in May 1845. I must therefore thank all those individuals who ensured I put in the extra research to enable me to answer their questions in a tolerably authoritative way.

I am indebted to all museums, libraries and online archive depositories, including Google, who have digitised so much public domain material in order to make it available to researchers. Impossible tasks are made possible by such work and our knowledge and understanding of the past is made richer as a result. I'm particularly indebted in this respect to the British Newspaper Archive and the British Library collection it holds. Searchable online resources mean that what might have taken years before can now be done in months.

I am enormously grateful to those among my friends and family who have put up with me while I recount tales of circuses, pantomimes and performers, many of which have not got into this book. A growing collection of tales that didn't make the book can be found on the companion website - www.theclownking.com, which came about in order satisfy the urge to go off at a tangent and share their stories as well.

Finally, I must give my sincere thanks to my wife, Janet. Despite a demanding job, she found time to proof read and edit the drafts. 'Thank-you' is rather inadequate.

Gareth H. H. Davies

Introduction

"The aim of microhistory is not simply to offer a biographical investigation of a particular person, but to probe the definitive features of the life in order to see what the case study reveals about the time and place. … the aim is to discover the special aspects of the individual, whose situation, actions, and beliefs provide the telling traces of cultural, social, moral and political conditions.[1]"

Arthur Nelson left no personal account of his life or diary to draw on. However, this successful Victorian clown left an archival trail of his career, from 1842 to 1860, through playbills and circus posters, newspaper advertisements and short reports of performances. These engagements provide a view into his life. However, when put together with other accounts and descriptions of the period, it is possible to gain some insight into what his world might have been like.

The period was one of rapid economic and social change in which forms of popular entertainment were not only growing but also adapting to these changes. In the comic world of the period, there was a significant hierarchy and Arthur Nelson was near the top as, "the successful comic man could work in the ring, the halls and pantomime; he went wherever space and pay was best.[2]".

This book is not a biography of Arthur Nelson. Any traditional biography of the man would have to rely on conjecture and therefore stray too far from being a true account of his life. However, where there is evidence, the book tries to glimpse the character of the man, and his interactions with both events and genres of the period. It is these intersections that provide the focus for the text.

---

[1] Postlewait, T. (2003) Micro-history and Writing of Theatre History Today (unpublished paper for the Historiography Working Group: IFTR/FIRT: Worcester, England, June 2003), cited in Bratton, J and Featherstone, A (2006) The Victorian Clown. p.32 n.56.

[2] Bratton, J. and Featherstone, A. (2006) The Victorian Clown. p.10.

1

The Theatrical Booth

We know relatively little of Arthur Nelson's early life. Born in Bristol to Henry Nelson, a musician, we do not know whether he came from a theatrical or circus family or where his father performed. We know from his obituary[1] that he worked first as an actor in provincial and minor theatres before becoming a clown. On the 2 August 1835, aged 19, he married Ann Moon at St John's, Westminster[2]. Ann was an equestrian performer[3] and from newspaper accounts often performed in the same arena[4]. By 1841, Nelson was performing as a 'comedian' with Parrish's Theatrical Booth[5] and was lodging with fellow performers in Sheffield at the time of the census[6] (6 June), perhaps in preparation for the Sheffield Fair that began on 9 June.

The largest fairs were in London and, by 1822, Bartholomew Fair had five circus booths, four menageries, a number of theatres, peep shows, freak shows, glass blowing acts and a number of exhibition shows. Henry Morley commented in 1859 that the price of admission to the larger, shows such as Wombwell's, Atkins and Richardson in 1830, was sometimes six times as much as the penny shows exhibiting at the fair[7]. By the early 1840s the fairground, originally an adjunct, had begun to dominate the old annual markets, particularly in industrialised towns such as Sheffield.

Sheffield, like other larger towns held two annual fairs, one at Whitsun and a November fair, or Saturnalia. Both were held over two days. The crowds were swelled by inhabitants from neighbouring towns as rail links made day excursions feasible. Indeed, in 1840, the North Midland Railway opened a temporary station at Beighton to provide easy access to the Sheffield Fair[8].

One Sheffield newspaper summed up the November fair:

"… our annual winter fair or Saturnalia was opened in earnest yesterday morning. To the many hundreds and thousands who have hoarded up their spare pence, which have in the majority of cases, we trust, been transformed into shillings … this festival is one of pleasure, more so,

RICHARDSON'S THEATRICAL BOOTH, BARTHOLOMEW FAIR
1808
Microcosm of London by Rudolph Ackermann, W. H. Pyne, William
Combe, Augustus Pugin, Thomas Rowlandson

however, to the juvenile portion of the population than the paterfamilias. … those who are fortunate enough to have money to spend have this week multitudinous ways and means of spending it. The fair ground and the surrounding neighbourhood is now daily crowded with people. This multitude in a very great measure comprises the majority of the mediocrity of the town residents, but their number is greatly augmented by our distant Yorkshire, Derbyshire, Lincolnshire, Nottinghamshire and Lancashire friends. These 'outsiders' do not know the town so well as our resident friends, therefore, we will at once chaperon them from the railway stations to the fair ground.[9]"

The large crowds inevitably attracted the criminal fraternity and The Sheffield Independent offered the following warning:

"THE FAIR. – Sheffield Fair commences on Tuesday, and we warn our readers to keep a sharp look-out after their houses and pockets. Countrymen too, will do well to guard against the 'sharp-swap' and 'pepper-gang[10]' gentry; and bear in mind some of the tricks which they performed at recent fairs, in making dishonest bargains and exchanges.[11]"

Indeed, in 1822 Henry Thompson and William Brammer were charged with picking the pocket of Thomas Myham at Sheffield Fair robbing him of a purse containing over twenty pounds[12]. Found guilty, they were both sentenced to death[13].

The fairground at Sheffield Fair included a large number of booths. These were temporary trading places, arranged in 'streets' and offered greater security than simple stalls. From the 17th century onwards they began to offer entertainments and housed performances and exhibitions of 'monsters', peepshows, and acrobats. For example, Wombwell's menagerie, showing a range of exotic animals, was a regular and popular booth that visited both the summer and winter fairs:

"WILD BEASTS. — It will be observed, from an advertisement in

DEATH OF THE "LION QUEEN" IN WOMBWELL'S
MENAGERIE, AT CHATHAM
Illustrated London News 19 January 1850, p.33.

another column, that Wombwell's royal menagerie is still exhibiting in the fair. We have paid a visit to the exhibition, and after witnessing the control exercised by the keepers, over the most ferocious animals of the bute creation, were highly gratified with a sight of the giraffe, or camel leopard, an animal never seen here before, but in Van Amburgh's collection. It is a tall and handsome quadruped, imported from the interior of Abyssinia, in Africa, and we are informed, was purchased by Mr. Wombwell, at a cost of £1,500. The scholars of the Lancasterian schools were yesterday gratuitously admitted, by Mr. Wombwell, to see the exhibition.[14]"

These menageries were also the origin of performance with exotic animals that became so much a part of later 19th and early 20th century circus entertainment. It was not without danger, as Ellen Bright, a seventeen year old performer with Wombwell's Menagerie, found to her cost in January 1850 while the show was at Chatham[15].

Another popular attraction was the travelling theatrical booth. The smaller affairs comprised of a makeshift stage with curtained area at the rear, but the bigger enterprises, such as Parrish's and Richardson's, were more elaborate structures with an open parade at the front and an indoor venue behind. Richardson's theatrical booth was said to be 30 metres (100 feet) long and 9 metres (30 feet) wide with an audience capacity of 1500 people[16]. Parrish's certainly had a canvas roof[17].

Peter Paterson provides an insight into how audiences at the fair were attracted to the performances: "… we mount to the outside, and strut about for perhaps half-an-hour or so, sometimes having a dance to music of our select band, the low comedian all the while (sometimes dressed as a pantomime clown) making as much fun as he possibly can by 'mugging,' or otherwise. Usually, all are dressed in a most exaggerated style, especially the 'comedy chaps,' in order to raise a laugh.[18]"

Nelson, would have been one of these 'canvas clowns'. Henry Mayhew interviewed one of his profession for the third volume of his book, London Labour and London Poor:

"A TALL, fine-looking young fellow, with a quantity of dark hair, which he wore tucked behind his ears, obliged me with his experience as a clown at the fairs …

"I first commenced some twelve years ago, at Enfield fair. It was a travelling concern I was with, – 'Thespian Temple', or Johnson's Theatre, – where I was engaged to parade on the outside of the walking gentleman. There was no clown for the pantomime, for he has disappointed us, and of course they could not get on without one; so, to keep the concern going, old Johnson, who knew I was a good tumbler, came up to me and said 'he had *nauti vampo*, and your nabs must *fake* it;' which means – We have no clown, and you must do it. So I done the clowning on the parade, and then, when I went inside, I'd put on a pair of Turkish trousers, and a long cloak, and hat and feathers, to play 'Robert duke of Normandy,' in the first piece.

"'You see the performances consisted of all gag. I don't suppose anyone knows what the words are in the piece. Everyone at a show theatre is expected to do general business, and you're short of people (as we was at Johnson's, for we played 'Robert duke of Normandy,' with three men and

CLOWN AT A FAIR, MAYHEW'S LONDON LABOUR AND
LONDON POOR
Mayhew, H. (1861) London Labour and London Poor Vol III, p.132.

two girls), Clown is expected to come on and slip a cloak over his dress, and act tragedy in the first piece. We don't make up so heavy for the clown for fairs, only a little dab of red on the cheeks, and powder on the face; so we've only just got to wipe off the 'slop' when it's in the way. You looks rather pale, that's all. The dress is hidden by the one we put over it. ...

"When we parade outside, it all depends upon what kind of Pantaloon you've got with you, as to what business you can make. When we first come out on the parade all the company is together, and we march round, form a half-circle, or dress it, as we say, while the band plays 'Rule Britannia,' or some other operatic air. Then the manager calls out, 'Now Mr Merryman state the nature of the performances to be given here today.' Then I come forward, and this is the dialogue: 'Well, Mr. Martin, what am I to tell them?' 'The truth, sir! what they'll see here today.' 'Well, if they stop long enough they'll see a great many people, I shouldn't wonder.' 'No, no, sir, I want you to tell them what they'll see inside our theatre.' 'Well sir, they'll see a splendid drama by first rate performers, of Robert Dooke of Normandy, with a variety of singing and dancing, with a gorgeous and comic pantomime, with new dresses and scenery, and everything combined to make this such an entertainment as was never before witnessed in this town, and all for the small charge of three shillings.' 'No, no, Mr. Merryman, threepence.' 'What! threepence? I shan't perform at a threepenny show.' And then I pretend to go down the steps as if leaving; he pulls me back, and says, 'Come here, sir; what are you going to do?' 'I shan't spoil my deputation playing for threepence.' 'But you must understand, Merryman, we intend giving them one and all a treat, that the working-classes may enjoy theirselves as well as noblemen.' 'Then if that's the case I don't mind, but only for this once.'

"'Then I begin spouting again and again, always ending up with 'to be witnessed for the low charge of threepence.' Then Pantaloon comes up to say what he's going to do, and I give him the 'nap,' and knock him back. He cries 'I'm down,' and I turn him over and pick him up, and say, 'And now you're up.' Then the company form a half set and do a quadrille. When they have scrambled through that, Clown will do a comic dance, and then some burlesque statues. This is the way them statues are done: I go inside and get a birch-broom, and put a large piece of tilt or old cloth round me, and stand just inside the curtains at the entrance from the parade, ready to come out when wanted. Then the male portion of the company get just to the top of the steps, and Pantaloon says to one of them, 'Did you speak?' He says, 'When?' and Pantaloon says, 'Now;' and the whole lot make a noise, hollowing out, 'Oh, oh, oh!' as if they were astonished, but it's only to attract attention. Then the gong strikes, and the trumpets flourishes, and everybody shouts, 'Hi, hi! look there!' Then, naturally all the people turn towards the caravan to see what's up. Then they clear a passage-way from the front to the entrance and back, and bring me forth with this bit of cloth before me. The music flourishes again, and they make a tremendous tumult, crying out, 'Look here! look here!' and when all are looking up I drop the cloth, and then I stand in the position of Hercules, king of Clubs, with a birch-broom across my shoulders, and an old hat on a-top of my wig. Then the band strikes up the statue music, and I go through the statues; such as Ajax defying the lightning, and Cain killing his brother Abel; and it finishes up with the fighting and dying Gladiator. As a finale I do a back-fall, and pretend to be dead. The company then picks me up and carry me, lying stiff, on their shoulders round the parade. They carry me inside, and shout out, 'All in to begin; now we positively commence.' They then drive everyone in off the parade. When the public have taken their seats then we come strolling out, one at a time, till we all get out on parade again, because the place isn't sufficiently full. It's what we call 'making a sally.' The checktakers at the door prevent anyone leaving if they want to come out again.

... This is the parade business that is most popular at fairs; we do a few other things, but they are much of a muchness.[19]"

Paterson then describes what happens next:

"... we proceed round to the stage, when the curtain draws up, and the 'grand performances' of the evening commence in earnest. The play and farce are repeated as often as the place fills, the time occupied by the performance varying from three quarters of an hour to an hour and a-half, so that by the time we have entertained three audiences, or on a Saturday night six, and then counted and received our shares, we are pretty tired, and in a glorious mood for a nice bit of hot supper which constitutes an elysium to the poor actor;[20]"

Mayhew's clown also describes how hard the company worked:

"It's very hard work; and I have worked, since being with Snuffy Johnson,

17

seventeen hours of a-day; but then we have not had so much to do on the outside. Sometimes I've been so tired at night, that I've actually laid down in my dress and never washed, but slept like that all night.[21]"

While Paterson's company gave the actors shares in the takings, with appropriate amounts taken out for expenses (wardrobe and fittings, ground rent and travelling), Mayhew's clown describes another payment structure:

"The general pay for a clown, during fairtime, is 5s. or 6s. a-day, but this usually ends in your moving on the first day; then 4s on the second, and, perhaps 3s. on the third. The reason is, that the second and third day is never so good as the first. The excuse is, that business is not so good, and expenses are heavy; and if you don't like it, you needn't come again. They don't stand about what you agree for; for instance, if it's a wet day and you don't open, there's no pay. Richardson's used, when the old man was alive, to be more money, but now it's as bad as the rest of them. If you go shares with a sharing company it averages about the same.[22]"

Arthur Nelson had chosen to become a clown before he joined Parrish's theatrical booth, and to be a talking clown at that. The 'talking clown' followed in the genre of the 'Shakespearean' clown and relied on wit and repartee for his act, reacting to heckling from the audience or poking fun at the politics and events of the day. Nelson's apprenticeship in the booth would have therefore stood him in good stead in preparation for his career between the circus ring and the pantomime stage.

---

[1] The Era — 26 August 1860, p.10. – "Death of Mr. Arthur Nelson, the Clown.

The Death of Mr Arthur Marsh Nelson, popularly known as the 'clown king,' took place at Burnley, on the 27th ultimo, and he was interred at the Burnley Cemetery a few days afterwards. He was born about the year 1811, and on his first introduction to the stage played the leading parts in the legitimate drama in provincial and minor theatres. He subsequently adopted the 'talking clown' as his vocation, and his repartees in the ring were often remarkable for their readiness and humour. He was a good musician, and his clever performances of the pine-sticks exhibited skill and, with which, he had cultivated the eccentric branch of the art he had adopted. At Vauxhall Gardens and at several of the minor metropolitan and provincial theatres he was a great favourite. His last appearance in London was at the Alhambra Palace a few weeks back, when he introduced the female horse-tamer to the public."

[2] London Metropolitan Archives, Saint John The Evangelist: Smith Square, Westminster, Transcript of Marriages, 1835 Jan-1835 Dec, DL/t Item, 091/068.

[3] Class: HO107; Piece: 1570; Folio: 415; Page: 22; GSU roll: 174804.

[4] Edinburgh Evening Courant — 06 April 1852, p.3. – "Yesterday evening an American equestrian company commenced a short season of twelve nights here, in the Amphitheatre, Nicholson Street. ... The corps comprises several performers of first rate ability, and unrivalled, perhaps, in their particular feats. ... Mr. Mackett. Mrs Nelson, Mlle Fanny, and Master Nelson, appeared in graceful and pleasing scenes of equitation ... The principal clown was Mr Arthur Nelson, whose mirth and humour enlivened the intervals, and who performed some airs on the rock harmonicon with admirable dexterity. A little clown, of six or seven years of age, also occasioned great amusement by his mirthful freaks." (Master Nelson and the 'little clown' could well be Alfred and or Alben Nelson, their sons, who would have been thirteen and eleven at the time of this performance. All four have the occupation of 'Equestrian' in the 1851 census (Ibid.)).

[5] Turner, J. (2000) Victorian Arena: The Performers, A Dictionary of British Circus Biography Vol II. cited in Bratton, J. and Featherstone, A. (2006) The Victorian Clown. p.140 n.237.

[6] Class: HO107; Piece: 1336; Book: 3; Civil Parish: Sheffield; County: Yorkshire; Enumeration District: 7; Folio: 43; Page: 12; Line: 8; GSU roll: 464282 – The census return shows nine young 'comedians' lodging at a public house in Duke Street. Apart from Arthur, his younger brother Henry is also there, together with two members of the Parrish family, George and Robert.

[7] National Fairground Archive website — http://www.nfa.dept.shef.ac.uk/history/shows/history.html (last accessed 10 May 2015).

[8] Sheffield Independent — 13 June 1840.

[9] Sheffield Daily Telegraph — 25 November 1874, p.3.

[10] 'Peppering' was a particular type of sting operated at horse fairs such as Sheffield. Two members of the pepper gang or 'gentry' would target a gullible out of town buyer who was not a regular visitor to the fair. The gang members would then haggle over a horse at a hugely inflated price within his earshot. When the 'purchaser' walked away in disgust, the 'owner' would then offer the horse to the buyer at a supposed 'knock-down' price. Once bought, the buyer would find the horse was actually worth very little.

[11] Ibid. 8. — 10 June 1843, p.8.

[12] Ibid. — 27 July 1822, p.3.

[13] Ibid. — 3 August 1822, p.2.

[14] Ibid. — 4 December 1841, p.8.

[15] Illustrated London News — 19 January 1850. p.34. – "On Saturday evening last, an inquest was held at the Golden Lion Inn, Chatham, before J. Hind, Esq., coroner for West Kent, touching the death of Ellen Bright, a young girl, aged 17 years, who was killed the previous evening by a tiger, in the establishment of Mr. George Wombwell, which had arrived in that town for exhibition on the preceding day. The deceased, who was denominated, 'the Lion Queen,' had the honour of performing before her Majesty some time since, at Windsor Castle; and as will be seen from the evidence, was going through the usual evolutions with a lion and tiger at the time she met with her melancholy death."

[16] Kennedy, D. (2010) The Oxford Companion to Theatre and Performance. p.197.

[17] Morning Post — 4 September 1838, p.4. – "The wind, which rose as the thunder storm decreased, was of great violence. The covering of Mr. Parish's theatrical booth was blown completely off and torn to ribbons. So violent a storm is not remembered by the oldest inhabitant of Oldham."

[18] Paterson, P. (1861) Glimpses of Real Life as Seen in the Theatrical World. p.93.

[19] Mayhew, H. (1861) London Labour and London Poor Vol III. p.126-129.

[20] Ibid. 17.

[21] Ibid. 18. p.130.

[22] Ibid.

2

Circus and Theatre

In 1768, a former Sergeant-Major in the 15th Light Hussars, Philip Astley, established a riding school on a fenced wayside field on Lambeth Marsh. Calling himself the 'English Hussar', he performed feats such as straddling two cantering and jumping horses, doing headstands on a pint pot on the saddle and a 'parody of riding by a foppish tailor'. He would charge 6d. admission or 1s. for a seat. Astley never referred to his entertainment as a circus, but called the arena, a 'circle' or 'amphitheatre'. His business soon grew and by 1777 he had a large wooden building by Westminster Bridge.

Astley's Amphitheatre defined the form of the modern circus[1] and others

ASTLEY'S AMPHITHEATRE 1808
Microcosm of London by Rudolph Ackermann, W. H. Pyne, William Combe, Augustus Pugin, Thomas Rowlandson

soon realised the potential of this new and lucrative form of entertainment.

A show consisted of daring equestrian acts and 'pantomimes' based on popular tales and events of the time, padded out with clowns, jugglers or acrobats. Astley, and those that followed him, would show daring equestrian skills to the full by exploiting suitable stories.

These 'circuses' became popular entertainment at the beginning of the nineteenth century, and their forms of entertainment not only amused crowds at fairs, but in major towns and cities. Today one imagines a big-top tent as being the basis of a touring troupe, but early nineteenth century circus proprietors either took a pre-fabricated wooden building or would build a new one in-situ, if performing in a town for several weeks.

It was the Cooke family that ran many of the most successful circuses of the time. Thomas, the founder of Cooke's circus dynasty, was an accomplished rider, acrobat and ropewalker. In November 1806 he fitted up a former iron foundry on the Southside of the Seagate in Dundee and called it 'Cooke's Olympic Circus'. The next year he opened his 'New Olympic Circus' in Virginia Street, Aberdeen. The business and family grew, and by 18 September 1830 his son, Thomas Taplin Cooke, and the whole family gave a special Royal Command Performance at the Royal Pavilion, Brighton. From that moment on, he and his descendants were able to include the word 'Royal' in their circuses' titles.

Thomas Taplin's circus was based in Glasgow and, like Astley's Amphitheatre in London, was a wooden, temporary structure. In September 1836 Thomas Taplin took his troupe to America. It was in Baltimore that a major setback befell them when, on 8 February 1838, the building was burnt to the ground and, although no-one lost their life, fifty-two of his horses were killed. With no insurance, he had lost everything and was ruined. He attempted to carry on with untrained American horses, but eventually had to return to Britain that year.

Thomas Taplin's sons began to re-build their father's business. In 1839, a "large and elegant" circus was built on a vacant piece of ground behind the York Hotel in Edinburgh[2] and performances began. This was followed by seasons in Dundee, Glasgow and Edinburgh again. In late 1840 they expanded by constructing another circus in Hull but returned to

Edinburgh in December 1841. The circus interior was fitted with a "most costly, complete and brilliant fashion with a magnificent gas-lit chandelier.[3]" It was during this Edinburgh season that the first mention of Nelson as a performer in a circus is made. On Thursday 24 March 1842, the first 200 people to the pit and gallery were to receive a full-length portrait of him[4].

In April the company returned to Aberdeen[5]. We can get a flavour of that 1842 Aberdeen performance from an autobiographical account written by A.S. Cook in 1911:

"To 'see' the circus was a great event, and was looked forward to by me with delight and expectation. Sealed in the pit, to which I was admitted at half-price, I surveyed the scene with interest. The boxes were in the centre, below which were entrances to the ring. The gallery was at the opposite end of the house from the pit, and had a passage leading from the arena to the top of the gallery. The large gasalier suspended from the roof of the building was brilliantly lighted, and was to me a surprise and attraction, and the light painted woodwork and a few simple draperies gave the interior a bright appearance.

At half-past seven precisely a bell rang for the commencement of the performance. I was all excitement as to what would be next, when a horse was trotted into the ring, followed by a lady, and accompanied by the

PLAYBILL FOR COOKE'S CIRCUS, YORK HOTEL, NICOLSON ST., EDINBURGH, FEBRUARY 1840
Library of Congress 99471609

merryman and the lady, who was lightly and gaudily dressed, mounted the steed and rode several times around the circle, the orchestra playing the while. A few minutes rest was given the equestrian, during which Charlton the clown, a funny little man, made himself conspicuous and the audience merry by jesting with the ringmaster and performing several clever and comic acrobatic feats. He was received with rapturous applause, and was evidently a great favourite.

"Another of the performances of that evening is still fresh in my memory, and I recall the scene as if it happened yesterday. The gasalier was lowered till it almost reached the ground. From the roof a rope was loosened, the ends of which were attached to beams in the roof – this was a slack rope. A ladder was brought into the ring, and Mr William Cooke, a singularly powerful and athletic looking man, clad in a spangled dress which shone like silver, ascended the ladder, and sitting astride on the rope began to swing backwards and forwards. When he reached the extremes on either side he turned heels overhead. He next went through the same performance while standing on the rope as it swung, then, steadying it while still standing, he turned, it was said, a hundred times with great velocity, giving his person the appearance of a silver wheel in rapid motion.

"The great event of the evening, however, was 'Mazeppa, or the Wild Horse of the Desert.' Mazeppa was acted by Alfred Cooke. He was tied with his back to that horse. The animal with its burden darted wildly into the supposed arena, and after a round or two dashed up the passage in the gallery, which was supposed to be a mountain, reappearing in a minute or so by the entrance below the side boxes, again running round and disappearing by the gallery, the enforced rider showing marks of blood upon his person. In addition to this there were other performers in the play, clad in various costumes and moving about so as to convey to my inexperienced mind a very realistic scene of a somewhat bewildering character. I had no idea of the story, but Mazeppa's helpless appearance on horseback was to me the most vital and enduring remembrance I have of this equestrian display.

"As I was accompanied by several school companions about my own age. Alfred Cooke was the hero of our talk. So was Charlton the clown. Attempts were made by us to imitate his posturing. He could stand on his head, walk upon his hands, leap like a frog with body bent and legs over his shoulders; and wounds and bruises not a few were the result of our unsuccessful efforts to succeed as young acrobats.[6]"

The story of Mazeppa was a particularly popular adaptation during this period. Originally a folk tale, and made famous in the period by a poem by Lord Byron, it was first adapted for the stage in 1831 by Henry M. Milner[7]. It tells the story of a Ukrainian warrior who travels to the Polish court and falls deeply in love with a Countess, who is married to a very much older man. He is discovered and punished by being sent back to the steppes of Ukraine strapped naked to the back of his white charger.

PLAYBILL FOR ASTLEY'S MONDAY, AUG. 20, 1838 LAST 6 NIGHTS OF MAZEPPA!
British Library B20073 84

A. S. Cook goes on to give his opinion of Arthur Nelson:

"Besides Merriman Charlton, there were two other clowns, Nelson and Wells, but neither of these were of much account. Nelson was no acrobat, nor a great jester. He played sweetly on the dulcimer and other musical instruments.[8]"

Although this young man's expectations of a clown were not met on this occasion, clowns held a complex and difficult role within the early and mid-nineteenth century ring as Bratton and Featherstone point out:

"In the ring as on the stage, the nineteenth-century clown was arranger of tricks and manager of audience attention; a tongue-in-cheek admirer, or an outright parodist, of dangerous and skilful spectacles, who worked from his personal relationship with the audience and their expectations, using not only slapstick, but back-chat, elaborate monologues, inventive costumes new and traditional songs and, any kinds of reference to the real world beyond. He worked with other performers, and mediated their feats fluently, and also safely, to the audience sitting around.[9]"

Nelson was to work for the Cookes many times during his career, and, while not the principal clown on this occasion, was a favourite with the audience.

Circuses not only performed in purpose-built amphitheatres but also in theatres adapted for their performances. For example, at Whitsun 1845 Nelson was with William Cooke's circus at the New Standard Theatre in Shoreditch.

"STANDARD. — The Whitsun visitors to this very pretty little theatre were entertained with an entire change of performances, the spirited managers, Messrs. Johnson and Nelson Lee, having engaged the troupe of Mr. Cooke, the equestrian, and who made their début on Monday evening to a densely crowded house. The performances commenced with a military spectacle, entitled, 'The Conquest of Tartary; or The Eagle Rider of Circassia, and her Monarch Steed of the Desert,' followed by some excellent scenes in the circle; the evening's amusements terminating with a grand entrée of twelve horses, entitled 'The Warrior's Dream.' The spectacle was produced under the direction of Mr. W. D. Broadfoot, and reflects the highest credit upon this gentleman, whose judgment in such matters has been frequently put to the test, when director of Astley's Theatre. Mr. Arthur Nelson, as Clown, and T. Swan, as Buffoon, kept the company in high spirits throughout the performances in the ring. We doubt not that the speculation of Messrs. Johnson and Lee will turn out considerably to their advantage.[10]"

Johnson and Nelson Lee had only just taken over the licence of The Standard Theatre and began organising circus and equestrian shows to take place during the summer season (May 15 to September 15). These additional shows provided revenue for the regular season, which ran the rest of the year. Nelson Lee was also to become a prolific pantomime writer, which kept clowns like Nelson, who moved between theatre and circus, in constant work. As Lloyd's Weekly put it in December 1849, while summing up the pantomimes in the city and provinces, "… Nelson Lee, who has a finger in every pie of every theatre of note …".

In order to accommodate a ring the theatre was specially adapted:

"THE NEW STANDARD THEATRE.

"The East-enders have now their Amphitheatre of Cirque Olympique, for equestrian performances, which the proprietors of the New Standard

COOKE'S ROYAL CIRCUS AT THE NEW STANDARD THEATRE,
SHOREDITCH
Illustrated London News 17 May 1845, p.320.

Theatre have just provided for, in a novel and ingenious manner.

"This little Temple of Drama was erected a few months since, on the site of twelve houses adjoining 'the Standard Theatre,' by Mr. John Gibson, for the proprietors, Messrs. Johnson and Nelson Lee. It faces the Terminus of the Eastern Counties Railway, in Shoreditch. The interior is of the horseshoe form, and a domed roof, a construction peculiarly well adapted for the transmission of sound. The proscenium is 30 feet wide by 30 feet in height, the auditory has a circle of ten private and fourteen public boxes, which, with the pit and gallery, will accommodate 2200 persons. It is lit by a cut-glass chandelier; the front of the two boxes are coloured in two drabs, relieved with gold mouldings, pilasters, equestrian medallions, &c.

"The equestrian performances were the holiday novelty of Monday last; but in the place of the stage; for which purpose the flooring is, by ingenious machinery removed upon a kind of railway, the proscenium boxes are made to recede, and a ring is presented 39 feet in diameter, wherein Mr. Cooke and his Stud first exhibited on Whit Monday. Our illustration is a scene from an Equestrian Spectacle, also then produced, and entitled "The Conquest of Tartary; or, The Eagle Rider of Circassia, and her Monarch Steed of the Desert!" wherein a Mrs. R. B. Taylor's performance is very striking.[11]"

The Era also noted this novel arrangement:

"We may here allude to the novelty of the arena, which is formed by the removal of a great portion of the stage, and the withdrawal of the proscenium boxes, thus making the ring within a foot in circumference of that at Astley's, and enabling the spectators, at the furthermost part of the house, to have a full view of the whole performances. Messrs. Arthur Nelson and Rochez were the Clowns in the ring.[12]"

Apart from in the circus ring, by the middle of the nineteenth century the clown had become the major role in theatre pantomimes. The English pantomime had developed from the Italian commedia dell'arte, and refined and transformed into the 'harlequinade' on the French stage. The harlequinade, had a regular cast of characters, Harlequin, Columbine, Pantaloon, Pierrot and Scaramouche. In the eighteenth century John Rich, at the Lincoln's Inn Fields Theatre and then at Theatre Royal, Covent

Garden, transformed this model into a distinctively English version. Producing and devising the show, as well as playing Harlequin, Rich linked the action of the harlequinade to an opening 'play' or story. He gave his characters magical powers and added music, dance, mime, acrobatics, as well as spectacle, special effects and topical allusions. Rich's adaptation retained Harlequin as the main character, with his black mask, cocked hat [13]and bat (slapstick). Rich's contribution was to provide the template for further adaptations:

"The theory of the pantomime invented, or rather adapted, by Rich, was this:— Harlequin was the lover of Columbine, Pantaloon was her father, and the Clown was the blundering servant of Harlequin. The harlequinade represented the courtship of harlequin and columbine, whose course of true love was prevented from running smooth by the constant interference of her father, pantaloon. The pantomime generally opened with the abduction of columbine from pantaloon's house. Pantaloon would discover his loss and follow in pursuit, and when overtaken, harlequin used his magic bat to play tricks upon the old man and defeat his purpose. In this the clown was the assistant and servant of harlequin, and his function was to delude and beguile the pantaloon while harlequin was courting his daughter. In the course of their adventures, columbine was often rescued by her father and taken back home; but was always carried off again by her lover, with whom she is at last made happy with the old man's consent. The bat, or wooden sword, was supposed to have the power of changing copper into gold, cutting people in half, and enabling harlequin to jump through stone walls and vault over the tops of houses. The four colours of his dress had a special meaning. The yellow indicated jealousy; the blue, truth; the scarlet, love; and the black, invisibility; and they stood at the same time as the emblems of fire, air, earth, and water.[14]"

If Rich had defined the form of the pantomime, it was Grimaldi who made the Clown the central figure of the show in the period 1806 to 1828:

"Grimaldi's clown was a Londoner in hyperbole: channelling its voracious consumerism and infusing his clowning with its manic energy, flamboyant theatricality and love of show... Grimaldi's clown was cunning, covetous and childlike in his wants, an uncensored mass of appetites and an embodied accumulation of unconscious desires. Everything tempted him, calling him forward and enticing him to touch, tinker and meddle, with an impetus that overrode all considerations, especially the law ... Londoners revelled in Grimaldi's lawlessness, watching him commit a litany of crimes that outside the theatre would have been rewarded with transportation or death. 'Robbery became a science in his hands', wrote one commentator, recalling with relish the way he would pilfer a leg of mutton and, with 'bewitching eagerness', extract handkerchiefs and pocket watches with 'such a devotion to the task' that he 'seemed imbued with the spirit of

THE TRANSFORMATION SCENE FROM THE ADELPHI CHRISTMAS PANTOMIME OF " MOTHER SHIPTON, HER WAGER ; OR, HARLEQUIN KNIGHT OF LOVE, AND THE MAGIC WHISTLE."—(SEE NEXT PAGE.)

TRANSFORMATION SCENE MOTHER SHIPTON, HER WAGER; OR, HARLEQUIN KNIGHT OF LOVE AND THE MAGIC WHISTLE, ADELPHI THEATRE 1857
The Illustrated London News 3 January 1857, p. 667.

peculation'.[15]"

During the period in which Nelson was performing in pantomimes, the performance essentially became two shows in one, with a 'transformation' taking place to divide the action. The transformation scene could take as long as twenty minutes and was central to the pantomime spectacle.

Through a romantic fairy-laden magic[16], elaborate lighting and mechanical devices, the actors in the performance were transformed into the characters of the harlequinade and scenes from the production parodied. The two acts usually had separate casts, with the clown, acrobats and other pantomimists restricted to the harlequinade.

We can perhaps understand what one of these performances was like by looking at the Pavilion Theatre's pantomime for the 1850 Christmas season in which Nelson played the Clown in the harlequinade.

The pantomime was entitled, 'Sugar and Spice and All Things Nice, or Harlequin March of Intellect and the Fairy Queen of the Blissful Realms':

"The opening on the present occasion commences with the Studio of Old Rackbrain, the original inventor of pantomimes, who is discovered wrapped in thought, surrounded by all the materials that have been called into action for all the pantomimes that were ever written. His is now, however, 'in a regular fix;' he cannot hit upon a single idea but what has been 'used up'. He thinks of times gone by, and thinks of prices too – and says: ——

'The managers could then, the cunning foxes,
Ask and have four shillings to the boxes;
But now the case is different quite,
With greater difficulties I have to fight;
For is no easy job, however, willing,
To provide a good entertainment for a shilling;
Or, if that price some pockets may not fit
The same performance may be seen for six pence in the pit,
And though the actors get no less in salary
Admission may be gained for threepence to the gallery.'

Almost driven to despair, he gives up all as lost; and by some smart and piquant lines the audience is worked up into a state of peculiar uncertainty, a la 'The Manager in Distress'; and the conclusion is there will be no pantomime at all. But such catastrophe must not happen in a progressive age like 1851, and he is relieved from his distress by the sudden and mysterious appearance of the March of Intellect, who, seeing Rackbrain scribbling to no purpose, exclaims:

'Stop your goose quill; your labour's vain, I fear,
And failure certain unless I interfere.'

The old author is greatly chagrined at the impertinence of the March of
Intellect, who tells the old man his day is past – that pantomimes of old
were very well in their way but the age wants something more racy and
novel, and that the March of Intellect is on the alert. The matter
discussed, a compact is entered into, the Spirits of the Age are at the
command of the March of Intellect, appear as here we have five of the
most gorgeous tableaux ever witnessed here at the east end of London,
representing the Genius of Painting, Music, Poetry, Sculpture, and
Mechanical Art. We are then conveyed to the shop of Sugar Candy who
has made some wonderful discoveries in the World of Sweets. He is in
possession of one fair daughter that he loves passing well, and whom he
intends to marry to one Mr. Fig, a retired West India merchant, very rich
and very old. Now this does not exactly coincide with the views of fair
Salina, Candy's daughter, who has chosen a husband for herself in the
shape of one Corney Carraway Comfort, who is the only comfort of her
life. The old boy being repulsed, then follows so sparkling and witty
dialogue on passing events, and old Fig, driven to despair, determines on a
visit to the Hall of Brazen Heads, which is inhabited by demons,
astrologers, and all sorts of unnatural genies. Here he invokes the aid of a
renown personage possessed of supernatural power, rejoicing in the name
of Bloodgame. This worthy promises Fig, for a consideration, to destroy
young Carraway, and he with satellites, depart the errand, but are thwarted
in their intent by the interposition of the good fairies, who watch over the
young lovers. They, however, in the hurry and confusion, seize the wrong
man, which venture gives to some comic scenes. The lovers eventually
changed into the usual pantomimic personages. The character of the
March of Intellect, which is well conceived, will be sustained by the
manager's daughter, Miss Sarah Thorne, a clever and rising young actress,
who it may be expected will render the pantomime's great feature. Mr.
Arthur Nelson, of stone harmonicon notoriety, is Clown; Herr Ruckman,
Pantaloon; Miss Butler and Miss Rosa Nathan, the two Columbines; and
Signor Charltoni and Howard Lewis, the two Harlequins. In conclusion we
may observe, the scenery is of magnificent description, and in every
department Mr. Thorne has been lavish in expense. A long run may be
consequently expected.[17]"

32

PANTALOON AND CLOWN
Halliday, A (1863), Comic Fellows; or The History And
Mystery Of The Pantomime: With Some Curiosities And
Droll Anecdotes Concerning Clown And Pantaloon,
Harlequin And Columbine, title page.

In all there were sixteen scenes in the production, equally divided by the 'transformation'. Of the characters, only the March of Intellect, Sarah Thorne, appeared in both acts. The scenes of the harlequinade often parodied those of the first act. For example, the tableaus presented in scene one and 'London Statues and Punch's Pose Plastiques'[18] in scene thirteen. Other scenes also provide an insight into how the pantomime script alluded to topical issues of the period. In scene nine, the first scene of the harlequinade, which takes place in butcher's and baker's shops, Pantaloon and Clown play Mr. Serag and Mr. Turnover. First, they begin by singing the patriotic ballad, 'The Roast Beef of England'[19], then the

Clown turns potato dealer and dinner time comes and there is no dinner[20]. Then there is bad news for the poor as the Bread Rises[21] in the baker's shop, followed by good news as the Corn Laws are repealed.

It is also this pantomime that gives us an insight into the character of Arthur Nelson. On one occasion, during scene eleven, Nelson assaulted the stage manager and found himself in court. The report of the case in the trade newspaper provides us with a description of the scene:

"ASSAULT UPON A STAGE MANAGER,

"NEALE v. NELSON. — This was an action, tried last Tuesday in the Whitechapel County Court, to recover the sum of £25, as compensation in damages for an alleged atrocious assault upon the person of Mr. Neale, the stage-manager of the Pavilion Theatre, by Mr. Arthur Nelson, the popular clown of that establishment. Mr. Metcalf appeared as council for the plaintiff, and Mr. Pelham informed the Court, with considerable gravity, that he had the honour upon this occasion to represent the Clown. The plaintiff having stated his version of the assault, Mr. Pelham said he had no doubt his Honour would like to hear the title of the Pantomime which gave rise to the feud upon which the action was founded. The plaintiff accordingly informed the Court that the production was entitled Sugar and Spice and all Things Nice – a title which seemed amazingly to tickle the risibility of the learned judge. The composition is by Mr. W.R. Thorne, the spirited lessee, and is said to possess very superior merit. It appeared from the evidence that one of the scenes, which is most ingeniously contrived, represents a moon of considerable magnitude, with movable eyes and capacious mouth. So far, therefore, the Pavilion moon may be said to take the shine out of its innumerable predecessors, being not merely a new moon, but a moon upon an entirely new principle. For past ages the glorious orb of night has been addressed as gentle, silvery, silent, and refulgent. Not only has she furnished a study for the pencil, but poets have sung her praises with melodious song, while many a languishing lover, whose malady had no doubt been influenced by 'something about the moon's rays,' has in solitary sadness, and with the utmost coolness imaginable, invited his 'fond one' to 'meet him by moonlight alone – a very pretty spee. But let that pass, in order to trace in another hemisphere a moonlight scene of deeper interest. Much that has been said of the Pavilion moon, it is not so much on account of her pale bewitching face that her superior qualities have been admired by the wise men of the east, as from the fact that her possessing that which no other moon was ever known to possess, namely, a voice of sweetest melody. And this singular gift it is that wins the affection of the Clown, who serenades her as follows: –

'Pray Mistress Moon are you going out?
You seem rather mystical – what's it about?'

In reply to this somewhat impertinent interrogatory, Mistress Moon invites the clown –

'To put a ladder to her face, and a shilling in her mouth.'

Pantaloon is delighted beyond measure, and he joins with great glee, in a trio with the clown and moon[22]. It so happens on one occasion, that Mrs. Moon fell into a state of somnolency, and refused to chant. The clown repeated his stanza, but she was silent as the night. The gods, as well they might be, were dreadfully enraged, and to assuage their anger the clown was compelled to retreat to the side scenes and sing to the moon. Indignant at this sort of treatment on the part of his faithless mistress, the clown, in a moment of excitement, called her a — thief. The expression reached the ears of the stage manager, who having some respect for the moon (Smith), said she was no more a thief than the clown, adding in allusion to that gentleman's peculiar line of character, that he was mere horsedung and sawdust[23]. Wereupon the clown became very much excited, and called the stage manager an infernal little Quilp[24], a comparison which was considered the more painful from the fact if its having reference to the manager's deformity. The storm grew higher, and the clown struck the manager, shook him, and threatened to knock him straight, an experiment which was, however, prevented by the arrival of the pantaloon.

"Such is an outline of the outrage which gave rise to the present action. Mr. Metcalfe's opening and Mr. Pelham's reply were exceedingly humorous, highly relished, and frequently applauded, and the various actors who were called upon to give evidence sustained their characters with zeal and ability. Three witnesses on the part of the defendant distinctly swore that the blow complained of was a mere tap with a forefinger, and this evidence was to a certain extent confirmed by Mr. Neale's surgeon, the substance of whose evidence went to show that, beyond being nearly frightened out of his wits, the worthy manager had sustained no material injury, there being no appearance of discolouration in any part of his face.

"In the eyes of the law, however, an assault had been committed, and for that offence his Honour ordered the defendant to pay the sum of £4 4s.[25]"

Nelson, like most well known clowns of his era, was caught between two social worlds. In the circus, it was the equestrians that held the highest status with their skill and daring. James Frowde, a clown with Hengler's circus, described how his circus colleagues received his first riding lesson:

"After much jeering and [being] called a tailor[26], I was allowed to fall to the rear, wondering whether all tailors off the board, and from behind the counter were on the saddle and outside the horse.[27]"

Indeed W. F. Wallett, a contemporary of Nelson, in his autobiography says, "As a rule clowns, acrobats and gymnasts and the like are bad riders.[28]"

In the theatre, the pantomime was seen as a lower art form to the play, and the actors in the harlequinade were regarded as lower status to those that performed in the first half of the production especially if, as Clown, they had a circus background. However, from his run-in with Fredrick Neale, we can tell that Arthur Nelson took pride in his work, and although perhaps hot-headed, was not about to be insulted by anyone.

The harlequinade and Clown were crucial to the success of the Victorian pantomime and audiences flocked to see them. Considered as family entertainment, a successful Christmas season might bring in up to 85 percent of a theatre's profit for the year[29]. Despite his low social standing in theatrical terms, this often meant that a popular clown could command higher wages than his thespian counterparts and demand incentives, such as benefit nights, in preference to others in the cast.

---

[1] See Rendall, M. (2014) Astley's Circus: The Story of an English Hussar.

[2] The Scotsman — 2 November 1839 – cited in McMillian, S. (2012) Cooke's: Britain's Greatest Circus Dynasty.

[3] McMillian, S. (2012), Cooke's: Britain's Greatest Circus Dynasty, p.24.

[4] Ibid.

[5] The Northern Figaro — 4 June 1898 in an article, "Circuses in the City from 1807 to 1897 by Harry S. Lumsden" cited in McMillian, S. (2012) Cooke's: Britain's Greatest Circus Dynasty. – "In 1842 Aberdonians were again glad to welcome back Mr Thomas Taplin Cooke. He opened Cooke's Royal Circus in Union Street during the month of April. … Mr William Cooke who was manager of the circus this season gave riding lessons to those that wished them."

[6] Bon-Accord — 21 May 1903, in an article, "Cooke's Circus: My First Visit" – A.S.C. A.S. Cook wrote a book entitled, "Aberdeen Amusements Seventy Years Ago", in 1911, where he recounts the same story – cited in, McMillian, S. (2012) Cooke's: Britain's Greatest Circus Dynasty.

[7] Henry M. Milner was a playwright and author of melodrama and popular tragedies. His most notable work was "The Man and the Monster; or the Fate of Frankenstein" which opened in July 1826, six months after Mary Shelley's book, "The Last Man" was published. He adapted Byron's 1819 poem in 1831.

[8] Ibid.

[9] Bratton, J. and Featherstone, A. (2006), The Victorian Clown, p.7.

[10] The Era — 18 May 1845, p.2.

[11] Illustrated London News — 17 May 1845, p.320.

[12] Ibid. 10 — 15 June 1845, p.6.

[13] Rich's Harlequin did not speak. When he wore his black mask, he was invisible to the other players on stage, and used his hat to show, "the various mood of his changeful spirit, When it was straight upon his head, with the edges turned up all round in the form of a diadem, it gave him an air of audacious defiance. A little on one side, with the corner drawn down towards the shoulder, it gave him a tender, graceful air and signified that he was waiting for columbine, and that love was busy with his thoughts. If both corners hung like drooping ears on each side of his mask, he had encountered or was anticipating some misfortune, and the spectator might fancy tears rolling down his black cheeks ; but if his spirit was elated with joy, both corners were cocked up with a swaggering, triumphant twirl that seemed to throw scorn in the teeth of fate." – Halliday, A ed. (1863), Comic Fellows or The History and Mystery of the Pantomime.

[14] Ibid. p.29.

[15] McConnell Stott, A. (2009) The Pantomime Life of Joseph Grimaldi. p. xxv–xxvi. cited in Richards, J. (2014) Harlequinade and the Golden Age of Pantomime – http://theibtaurisblog.com/2014/12/19/harlequinade-and-the-golden-age of pantomime/ (accessed 12 May 2015).

[16] Fairy culture was ubiquitous to pantomime beginning in the 1840s – "The fact that pantomime of the forties stressed the fairy element … was cultural in origin, European as well as English, and by no means an isolated phenomenon. Victorian pantomime at Christmas was mostly for children and their families, and Victorian children and many adults – believed in fairies" – Booth, M. (1991), Theatre in the Victorian Age cited in n.4. Smith, J. Victorian Theater in the 1850s and Transformation of Literary Consciousness, Chapter 5: Tredennick, B (ed) (2011) Victorian Transformations: Genre, Nationalism and Desire in Nineteenth Century Literature. p.83.

[17] Lloyd's Weekly Newspaper — 22 December 1850, p.9 – 10.

[18] Pose plastiques were interpretations of statues posed by live performers and a popular entertainment in this period. For more information see chapter 7.

[19] "The Roast Beef of Old England" is an English patriotic ballad written by Henry Fielding for his play The Grub-Street Opera, which was first performed in 1731. The lyrics were added to over the next twenty years. The song increased in popularity when given a new setting by the composer Richard Leveridge who worked with John Rich at Lincoln Inn Fields. It became customary for theatre audiences to sing it before, after, and occasionally during, any new play.

[20] A reference to the Irish Potato Famine of 1845-52.

[21] A reference to the price of bread following the implementation of the Corn Laws, which kept bread prices artificially high. The Corn Laws were repealed in 1846 leading to the fall and stabilisation of the price of bread.

[22] According to the theatre playbill, they sing the song, 'Buffalo Gals can't you come out tonight', an American ballad written and published as 'Lubly Fan' in 1844 by the blackface minstrel John Hodges, who performed as Cool White. The song was widely popular throughout the United States. The lyrics were often changed to suit the local audience, so it might be performed as 'New York Gals' in New York City or 'Boston Gals' in Boston or 'Alabama Girls' in Alabama:

"As I was rambling down the street, down the street, down the street,
A beauty gal I chanc'd to meet, Lovely as morning dew.
Buffalo gals, can't you come out tonight?
  can't you come out tonight?
  can't you come out tonight?
Buffalo gals, can't you come out tonight
And dance by the light of the moon.

Chorus:
Buffalo gals, can't you come out tonight?
  can't you come out tonight?
  can't you come out tonight?
Buffalo gals, can't you come out tonight
And dance by the light of the moon.

I said, 'My angel, will you talk?
And take with me a little walk,
With those sweet feet I view?'
    Buffalo gals, etc.

'And would you like to take a dance?
Quadrille, or Polka, fresh from France,
They're all alike to me.'
    Buffalo gals, etc.

'O! I will love you all my life,
And you shall be my happy wife,
If you will marry me.'
    Buffalo gals, etc."

[23] Joe Grimaldi had established the comic persona of the clown as a greedy and gluttonous thief. Illustrations of clowns during the period typically show three props to exemplify this fact – a string of sausages, a goose and a fish, bulging out from his pockets. The second insult refers to Nelson's circus background, which was thought inferior to acting on the stage.

[24] Daniel Quilp is the primary villain in Charles Dickens' 'Old Curiosity Shop' published in 1841. – "The child was closely followed by an elderly man of remarkably hard features and forbidding aspect, and so low in stature as to be quite a dwarf, though his head and face were large enough for the body of a giant. His black eyes were restless, sly, and cunning; his mouth and chin, bristly with the stubble of a course hard beard; and his complexion was one of that kind that never looks clean and wholesome. But what added most to the grotesque expression of his face, was a ghastly smile, which, appearing to be the mere result of habit and to have no connection with any mirthful or complacent feeling, constantly revealed the few discoloured fangs that were scattered in his mouth, and gave him the aspect of a panting dog."

[25] The Era — 2 March 1851, p.10.

[26] Tailor was the circus term for non-rider, or incompetent rider. Philip Astley's first performances included a 'parody of riding by a foppish tailor' or 'The Tailor of Brentford' in which he would pretend to flop and fall about his horse much to the amusement of the crowd. The story is taken from an account of a tailor who was riding to Brentford to vote in an election and has many mishaps on the way with his horse. In Astley's performance he has many false starts and falls, but finally succeeds and is revealed as a champion horseman.

[27] Ibid. 9, p.50.

[28] Wallett, W. F. (1884) The Public Life of W. F. Wallett, the Queen's Jester: An Autobiography of Forty Years Professional Experience & Travels in the United Kingdom, The United States of America (including California), Canada, South America, Mexico and the West Indies etc. p.29.

[29] Ibid. 16.

3

Wagers and Benefits

During the nineteenth century, and earlier, the opportunities available for performers, whether theatre, circus, or otherwise were limited. Those who came from a performing background rarely made a fortune or retired wealthy. Some of the great theatre and circus proprietors did enjoy a comfortable middle-class living[1], while many went bankrupt more than once[2] and left their families in destitution. Those that relied on their physical strength, such as acrobats, tumblers and clowns that performed stunts in the ring, naturally lost their suppleness as they got older, and therefore their ability to compete against younger men coming up. Some tried to move into management, including Arthur Nelson, often with mediocre success, or found themselves moving down the pecking order, back to the theatrical booths, or worse, to be 'penny-gaff' clowns[3] or street performers. Clowning was a hard physical life, and a heavy drinking culture inevitably existed in their world. Contemporary clowns, such as Tom Barry[4] and Richard Flexmore[5], died penniless often from drink related diseases[6].

Wages for performers such as Nelson varied[7]. For example, the 'penny circus jester' in his interview with Henry Mayhew suggested:

"Some jesters at circuses get tremendous engagements. Mr. Barry, they say, had 10l. a-week at Astley's; and Stonealfe, with his dogs, I should think is equal to him. There's another, Nelson, too, who plays on the harmonicon, and does tunes on bits of wood ... he's had as much as 15l a-week on a regular travelling engagement.[8]"

However, wages were nearly always supplemented by the benefit system that operated throughout the industry. A performer's 'benefit' meant that he or she would get the profit from that night's performance. Peter Paterson did not think much of the system:

"I never myself took a benefit, but cannot help saying that I think the benefit system a bad one; it quite destroys an actor's independence; and the taking of a benefit is one of the great causes of an actor being so frequently seen in public houses — it is in these places he 'makes' his ben.

He is obsequiously civil to all he sees, and appears profoundly grateful when any one takes a pit ticket from him; in fact, he has to sink his independence in order to sell tickets. Then he torments all his friends to sell for him; if he is slightly in debt to his baker or butcher, these unfortunate tradesmen are at once saddled with a score of pit, a dozen of stall, and fifty gallery cards. He must sell most of them, it is the best chance he will have of obtaining payment of his little debt. If the bénéficiaire be a freemason, he attends the free-and-easies of the lodge, and sings, and otherwise tumbles, in hope of patronage. A patronage is the grand hope of the actor, as an occasional bespeak is to the country manager. No stone is left unturned to obtain the colonel and officers of a regiment, if it be a garrison town; even a volunteer band is a godsend; and in this way a few pounds may be sometimes added to the actor's precarious income. Often enough the actor only works for the manager, the receipts not being enough to divide.[9]"

Despite Paterson's scepticism, benefit nights were part of the performance culture of the period and popular performers were regularly supported on their nights. Clowns such as Nelson, Swan, Barry and Twist had a distinct advantage as the funny men of their age, and devised ways in which they could ensure packed houses for their benefit night wherever they were. The offer of a 'Merry Andrew' in 'mumming attire' doing something to amuse the public for free would inevitably draw a huge crowd. Even better if a wager was involved to spice up the hour. The special rapport that clowns held with their audience could be transferred outside the ring or theatre and ensure that the public's expectation for laughter and fun at that night's show would be fully met.

The first recorded instance of these stunts occurred in July 1818, although no doubt such events had happened before:

"Thursday, Mr. Usher, the Clown at Astley's, undertook to go from Blackfriars-bridge to Westminster-bridge, in a washing tub drawn by four geese! He started with the tide at half past one, and accomplished the singular wager in one hour. An immense number of persons witnessed the undertaking when, after completing it he sailed to Cumberland-gardens and there offered, for a wager of 100 guineas, to return from thence through the arch of London-bridge, but no person would accept the challenge.[10]"

Dicky Usher's performance also involved cats and a decade later he had the opportunity to incorporate them as well:

"BRIGHTON The Rival Cats. — A singular wager took place last evening between Signor Cappelli, who is now exhibiting his wonderful cats at 95, St. James's-street, and Mr. Usher, the eccentric clown of Drury-lane, now performing in our theatre. The wager is for ten sovereigns, that Signor Cappelli's cat will draw, hand over hand from the bottom of his well, in his little bucket, six quarts of water in less time than Mr. Usher, the clown, will drive his stud of cats, four in hand, himself riding in the vehicle, a distance of 600 yards on the turnpike-road. — (Brighton Gazette.)[11]"

Soon these stunts were combined and became so well known that they did not have to be performed, simply referred to, in order to draw crowds to the theatre:

"THE GRAND NIGHT.

THE first appearance of Miss Charlotte USHER,
in her Six Characters; first appearance of Miss. M. A. PINCOTT, of the
Theatre Royal Drury-lane; the first night of the INDIANS and the
CHINESE; first night of the New Comic Pantomime of HARLEQUIN
IN IRELAND; and for this night only Mr. USHER will, by particular
desire, produce his

CELEBRATED STUD OF REAL CATS,
which he will drive Four in hand, several times round the Stage; with all
the other amusements.

FOR THE BENEFIT OF MR. USHER, CLOWN,

On FRIDAY, Aug. 29,

And last night but one of his appearance at this Theatre.

By desire of numerous Persons, who witnessed Mr. USHER'S eccentric Aquatic Excursion, in triumph, like Neptune in his Car, on the Thames, drawn by his four favourite Geese, Gibble, Gabble, Gobble, and Garble; then proceeding on the High-road, from Waterloo Bridge to the Royal Coburgh Theatre, London, drawn by his four thorough bred Mousers, who won the Wager, by galloping with Mr. Usher, in his little Carriage, 95 yards, within eight minutes and a quarter, on the Turnpike-road at Liverpool — he will, this night, mount his Car, and drive his favourite

CATS, 4 IN HAND,
Full speed, several times round the Stage.

Here go, gallop and trot,
Tibby, Tabby, Toddle and Tot — USHER.

The Performances will commence with the popular Melo Drama of

THE BLIND BOY.

Also, for the first time, the truly laughable, imitative piece, (in which Miss C. Usher had the honor of appearing before their Majesties, who were pleased to testify the highest admiration of her abilities,) called the

DAY AFTER THE FAIR,
In which Miss C. Usher will perform six characters.

The Performance will be relieved by the exertions of Mr. Usher, who will represent those singular Performers,

THE INDIANS AND CHINESE;
And give his imitation of the Feathered Tribe, accompanying the Band in

a

GRAND CANARY CONCERT.

By desire Mr. Bedford will sing 'Norah the Pride of Kildare.'

The whole to conclude with Mr. Usher's new Comic pantomime,
under the title of
Love, Hope, and Cupid; or, Harlequin in Ireland.

Those Ladies and Gentlemen who honor Mr. Usher with their interest and support, will please to observe, that to give scope to the Eccentric Performance of Mr. Usher with his Cats — at the conclusion of the Entertainments in the Theatre, he will drive his thorough-bred Mousers several times round the Stage.[12]"

Usher's antics were soon copied, often without care:

"DISGRACEFUL AFFAIR. — At Queen-Square, on Tuesday, a gentleman, residing at Pimlico, stated the following circumstances to the Magistrates: —On Monday, a bill was circulated, announcing certain performances to take place during the week at the Orange Theatre, Queen-st., Pimlico. A person named Lynch, was to be clown, and, prior to appearing on the stage, he was to drive in coach, drawn by four cats, named, 'Tibby, Tabby, Toddle, and Tot,' from the White Hart, King's-road, to the Orange Theatre, for a certain wager. On Monday evening, a fellow dressed as clown, appeared at the appointed place in a kind of a car, with four cats fastened to it. A large mob was in attendance, and a number of men belonging to the Theatre commenced pushing on the car as fast as they could. Three of the poor cats were torn to pieces in a short time, and the other was pushed along insensible. The cats, which had been borrowed from various persons, were sent home dead. The gentleman said similar proceeding would take place again that night. — The Magistrates gave directions to several officers to prevent it.[13]"

It was, however, Arthur Nelson who made the geese and washing tub stunt his own and it was at that first appearance with Cooke's circus in Aberdeen in 1842 where he probably did it for the first time.

"On 16th June Mr Nelson, one of the clowns of the circus, created quite a sensation by a novelty he introduced on the date of his benefit. He announced by handbills that he was to navigate the harbour from the lower basin to Regent Bridge in a tub drawn by two geese. This had the effect of exciting the curiosity of an immense crowd; many thousands of both sexes lined the quays long before the hour of the exhibition at half past 4 p.m. At an early hour respectable tradesmen, shopkeepers, learned lawyers, pious divines, sober matrons and prude old maids, and a large number of boys and girls, might have been seen making their way down the quays from all quarters of the town, and from every avenue to see this wonderful sight. All bridges and spots where a good view could be obtained were one black mass; no launch of the largest of our ships from Aberdeen harbour ever saw such a crowd as that day turned out to see the clown and his geese. When Mr Nelson arrived dressed in the costume of a merry-Andrew, and driving the geese before him with a long stick, he informed the spectators he would be unable to go the route he proposed, as the wind was contrary. However he sailed up the river in a boat, and let out from the bridge. He thus satisfied the curiosity of his mass multitude, and the advertisement had the effect of filling Cooke's Circus in the evening.[14]"

Nelson's experience in Aberdeen showed him that for the cost of a few handbills and posters, and an hour's free entertainment, he could fill his benefit evening to capacity.

In the next few years, the geese 'trick' became Nelson's signature when it came to drumming up a crowd for his benefit night. Indeed, one might suspect that it was almost expected of him in the places where the geography was suitable. However, it was not without problems. On 22 May 1844, Nelson performed the stunt from Park wharf to Broadwick's wharf, on the canal at Kidderminster where, "the crowd who were assembled threw pieces of bread to the geese, to divert their attention, and some threw stones and sticks at them. This, of course, rendered the task more difficult, but it was performed by Mr. Nelson in beautiful style.[15]"

There were other inherent risks with the stunt since most waterways and rivers were heavily polluted, something that Nelson was only too aware of.

"Yesterday afternoon week from 20,000 to 30,000 persons assembled on the banks of the Irwell, in Manchester to see Nelson, the clown,

PAVILION THEATRE, WEDNESDAY 2ND, APRIL 1851 FOR THE BENEFIT OF ARTHUR NELSON
© Victorian and Albert Museum, London

embark in a tub at the Preston-gardens, to be drawn by geese. About one hundred yards before completing his task his tub upset, and he was ducked overhead in a liquid smelling of anything but lavender or Eau de Cologne.[16]"

A ducking could be regarded as an occupational hazard, but if the crowd believed they had been misled things could get ugly. Tom Barry the clown (who was also renown for the same stunt) and was on contract with Nelson, and a third clown called Twist, at Astley's Amphitheatre found this to his cost in October 1844:

"A STALE JOKE. — Old father Thames was on Friday again the scene of much bustle and excitement, Mr. Barry, one of the clowns at Astley's Theatre, having a second time announced he would sail from Vauxhall to Westminster-bridge in a washing tub drawn by four geese. To add to the attraction of this strange feat it was stated that Mr. Carter, the 'Lion King,' would follow the clown in an open boat with one of his beautiful tigresses. In the latter respect, however, the spectators were disappointed, for no tigress was to be seen. By an alteration in the plan originally agreed upon thousands of persons were deceived. On account, it was said, of the tide, the clown sailed from the Red-house, Battersea, to Vauxhall-bridge,

BARRY THE CLOWN ON THE THAMES, 1844
Illustrated London News 28 September 1844, p.193.

instead of from the latter to Westminster-bridge. The crowd was on this occasion much greater than on the previous occasion. The whole distance from Westminster-bridge to a spot opposite the Red-house was lined with people, while an immense number collected on the wharfs on the opposite shore. At 5 o'clock Mr. Barry embarked in his 'frail vessel,' the geese being regularly yoked to it in shafts, and thus he proceeded driving 'four in hand,' amidst the laughter and cheers of innumerable water-parties preceding or following him, and the music of a large brass band playing 'Rule Britannia', and 'See the conquering Hero comes'. Some mischievous fellows caused the buffoon some uneasiness by endeavouring to 'foul' him and his geese, that is, to run against him with their boats, but the clownship was on the look out for such attacks, and escaped without injury. At Vauxhall he got into a common boat and rowed to Westminster, where the crowd, expecting to see him arrive with his tub and geese gave vent to their displeasure in that kind of hissing vulgarity termed 'goose,' and Mr. Barry got into the theatre with all possible speed.[17]"

It was this event that caught the attention of political satirists:

"THE GEESE ON THE THAMES

We regret to say that the LORD MAJOR and civic authorities, jealous of the attraction of MR. BARRY in his washing tub drawn by geese, which threaten to extinguish the glories of swan-hopping day, have forbidden all such exhibitions in the future. We believe, however, that the inventive person, MR. RICHARD LAMBERT JONES to MR. GIBBS that it would have a famous effect if, instead of using the LORD MAYOR's barge, in the next civic water party, MR. GIBBS were to allow himself to be drawn in a tub by four of his supporters chosen from the Court of Aldermen. SIR PETER LAURIE is all a-gog for the scheme, and there is a tremendous competition among the members of the court for the honour of appearing in harness. SIR PETER will, of course, take the place of one of the leading ganders.[18]"

The London crowds could not get enough of these exhibitions and within three days Nelson, and his companion clown Twist, for their 'joint benefit', decided to conduct a race:

"The CLOWNS' SAILING MATCH. — The third of these, what at one period was considered to be an undertaking of very great novelty, that of a person being pulled or drawn down the river by means of four geese being attached to a washing tub, came off on the river, between the Red-house, Battersea, and Vauxhall-bridge, on Monday afternoon. As this was the third within a fortnight, undertaken by persons connected with Astley's Theatre, something of the novelty had declined, when for the purpose of exciting the taste in the public, it was announced, that upon this occasion A. Nelson and Twist, the pantaloon and clown, would each make a voyage in different washing-tubs drawn by their respective teams; this announcement, accordingly drew together a large assemblage of persons at the Red-house, when, after a lapse of half an hour, the two aquaties, in full dress, namely, their theatrical costume, took their seats, and having picked up their reins, they each fired a pistol, when the medley procession started. They were accompanied by about 20 boats, which formed a kind of circle round the geese and tubs, and having gained the middle of the stream they floated down to Vauxhall-bridge which was reached by half-past five o'clock. After getting about 200 yards through the bridge, the two washing tubs were brought up to a barge, when Nelson and Twist got out of their craft, and each putting on a great coat, were conveyed to Lyon's yard, Stangate, where they were landed. On the passage down the water was very rough, and as the tubs passed by the above-bridge steamers, the surf from them caused the tubs to perform certain motions which appeared not to be quite agreeable to the heroes of the ring of the Amphitheatre. The original intention was to land at Westminster-bridge, but which was very wisely prohibited by the police as on the first of these novel undertakings, the mob in the Palace-walk was so great, coupled with the disturbances and robberies, that it was deemed advisable to prevent repetition. Whatever effect it produces for Nelson and Twist (that night being their joint benefit) it was attended with beneficial results for the proprietors of Vauxhall-bridge, as at the time the party passed beneath it, there could not have been less than 2,000 persons on the bridge, straining their eyes to catch a glimpse of the washing-tubs, geese, and buffoons.[19]"

As epitomised by this ballad, supposedly published in 1847, the stunt entered the popular culture which entertainers like Barry and Nelson not only drew on, but also were part of:

"Barry his four Geese and Washing tub.

Such funny games upon the Thames,
I'm sure you did see never,
There's Barry in his washing tub,
A driving on the river,
With four geese in harness fine;
Reined up so snug and tidy,
Gee up gee wo along they go,
Upon the Thames on Friday.

CHORUS

Such funny games upon the Thames,
Before you did see never,
Barry drives four geese in a washing tub,
So nicely on the river.

You may understand now four in hand,
To drive he does engage sir,
See up gee woe oh what a show,
And I will bet a wager,
Next Tuesday week that he'll complete,
Or I will swallow a donkey,
Will drive along thirteen tom cats,
A Magpie, pig and a donkey.

Some thought to france he would advance,
As I to you will pen then,
With his four geese add washing tub,
To fetch the king of Frenchmen.
And if he had as sure as mad
He would drive along the king sir,
In his tub and four, twelve mile an ho
From Portsmouth in to Windsor.

Next Monday there w ll be a lark,
Wilson and Twiss so clever,
Are going to drive a team a piece,
So neatly on the river,
Four geese a piece in a washing tub,
For a wager I declare sir's,

50

Then jump upon the geeses backs,
And mount into the airs sirs.

To see the Clown they do flock down,
With smiles on every feature,
From Vauxhall bridge to westminstere,
Then into the theatre,
See Batty with his four in hand,
In a washing tub so clever,
Along so go, gee up gee wo
So neatly on the river.[20]"

Barry and other clowns used the geese stunt to their advantage. However, it was Nelson that persisted with it for the totality of his career and, if we believe his publicity, by May 1857, he had completed the trick some 334 times[21]. It would seem that these drew huge crowds and added to his popularity. Indeed, at Perth on 3 November 1842 the onlookers equalled if not exceeded that for the Queen's visit to Taymouth a few months earlier[22]. However, it was his performance at Great Yarmouth in May 1845, that, in hindsight, he most probably regretted.

---

[1] For example, Bertram Mills died in 1838 – Western Morning News — 7 July 1838, p.3. – "Mr Bertram Mills, the famous circus proprietor, who visited Plymouth a few years since, left estate of the gross value of £146,574, with a net personalty £100,528 (Estate duty, £20,957). Probate has been granted to his widow, Mrs. Ethel Kate Mills, and his sons, Cyril Bertram and Bernard Notley Mills."

[2] For example, Alfred Eugene Cooke (1845-1900), son of Alfred Cooke was made bankrupt three times, see McMillian, S. (2012) Cooke's: Britain's Greatest Circus Dynasty, p.51-72.

[3] Henry Mayhew's interview with a 'penny-gaff' clown revealed he had given up clowning in theatres due to an injury, and become a pantaloon. – "Since the beginning of this year (1856) he had given up clowning, and taken to pantalooning instead, for 'on last boxing-day,' he informed me, 'he met with an accident which dislocated his jaw, and caused a swelling in the cheek as if he had an apple inside his mouth.' This he said he could conceal in his make up as a pantaloon, but it had ruined him as a clown." – Mayhew, H. (1861) London Labour and London Poor Vol III. p.121.

[4] Sheffield Daily Telegraph — 31 March 1857, p.2. – "DEATH OF BARRY THE CLOWN. — On Thursday night last, Mr. T. Darry, who was popularly known in performance of his duties as clown at various metropolitan theatres, died suddenly. Mr. Barry was, it is stated, in very reduced circumstances, and his demise occurred immediately after a benefit for his relief. His fate in this respect bears a strange similarity to those of many persons who have figured in the theatrical world." The day before William Cooke had given a benefit for his support at Astley's and The Allied Circus performing in Bristol had done likewise.

[5] The Era — 2 September 1860 – "The Late Richard Flexmore, The mortal remains of this very popular and greatly respected Pantomimist were consigned to their last resting-place on Monday last, at Kensall-green (a few paces from the spot that contains the ashes of the late M. Soyer), when a large number of his early friends, and gentlemen connected with the profession, attended to pay their tribute of respect to his memory. Since the suggestion that was thrown out by Mr. Boleno appeared in our last number, we have received numerous letters, testifying the readiness of the writers to co-operate in a benefit for the aid of the widow and the mother. It will, however, be gratifying to learn that, though the deprivation of; his income, consequent upon the long illness he had gone through had seriously reduced his circumstances, it is not thought necessary to call upon that aid, always so generously offered and so promptly afforded on these occasions, to contribute a fund for those he has left behind. The widow of Flexmore – known to the public as Madame Auriol – has undertaken to provide for the aged mother of the deceased; and for herself, she feels that whilst she can exert her professional talents she has no right to tax the hard earnings of others. But it would be taken by her as a most kindly and gracious recognition of the worth and talent of her late husband, if those who so readily came forward to proffer pecuniary aid in the hour of need would by subscription raise a sum to erect a Monument over his grave." Richard Flexmore died from atrophy on 20 August 1860.

[6] Newcastle Guardian and Tyne Mercury — 22 February 1868, p.7. – "PANTOMIMIC CHRONOLOGY IN THE NINETEENTH CENTURY. … 1857 – Tom Barry, clown, died in July of this year. His premature demise was accelerated through his own folly in giving way to inordinate drinking bouts. He was celebrated for a famous mock election speech, which he delivered upwards of 20,000 times in the course of his life, often four times a day while tenting with W. Batty."

[7] The Era — 18 April 1858 p.10. – "PABLO FANQUE AND HIS CLOWN, ARTHUR NELSON … In September last, Pablo Fanque engaged the mimic at a salary of £7 per week … Nelson, who has a £10 per week engagement at Ipswich …"

[8] Ibid. 3, p.134.

[9] Paterson, P. (1861) Glimpses of Real Life as Seen in the Theatrical World. p.46-47.

[10] Morning Post — 06 July 1818, p.3.

[11] Ibid. — 14 August 1829, p.3.

[12] Southern Reporter and Cork Commercial Courier — 26 August 1834, p.3.

[13] Bell's Life in London and Sporting Chronicle — 13 May 1832, p.4.

[14] The Northern Figaro — 4 June 1898 in an article, "Circuses in the City from 1807 to 1897 by Harry S. Lumsden" cited in McMillian, S. (2012) Cooke's: Britain's Greatest Circus Dynasty.

[15] Bristol Mercury — 25 May 1844, p.6.

[16] Hull Packet — 27 April 1855, p.7.

[17] West Kent Guardian — 19 October 1844, p.2.

[18] Punch or the London Charivari — July 1884, p.191. – Richard Lambert Jones was Chairman of the Improvement Committee of the City of London. His chairmanship included the rebuilding on London Bridge in 1831 and the Royal Exchange in 1844; Mr. Gibbs refers to Michael Gibbs who was elected Lord Mayor of London in 1844 and whose nickname was 'Gobble Gibbs' due to rumours of financial irregularities during his tenure; Sir Peter Laurie's political career began when he was elected Sheriff in 1823. He campaigned for the better treatment of prisoners and wrote two books on the subject. In 1826 he was elected alderman for Aldergate and became Mayor in 1832. The character of Alderman Cute in Charles Dickens' story The Chimes (1844) is a satirical representation of Laurie and his (as Dickens saw it) dismissive attitude towards London's poor. Read more at http://heritagearchives.rbs.com/people/list/peter-laurie.html.

[19] Ibid. — With regard to the last remark, the Vauxhall bridge in London was a toll bridge and would have charged the people watching to cross.

[20] From materials on loan to the National Library of Scotland from the Balcarres Heritage Trust see http://digital.nls.uk/74896102 (last accessed 14 May 2015). The reference to Wilson and Twiss is most likely a corruption of Nelson and Twist.

[21] Bradford Observer — 21 May 1857, p.1.

[22] Kendal Mercury — 17 December 1842, p.4.

4

Disaster at Great Yarmouth

In January 1845, when William Cooke, son of Thomas Taplin, applied to the Major of Great Yarmouth, Norfolk, "for leave to erect an amphitheatre, on the Theatre Plain[1]" he had no idea that his visit to Yarmouth would end in tragedy. He had set up his own touring circus in late 1843. During that first year he had taken the troupe to Norwich, and had returned to the city at the beginning of 1845 to an appreciative audience:

"The lovers of equestrian sports may enjoy a treat, by visiting the royal circus of Mr. Cooke at the Ranelagh gardens. We are informed the company is not to be surpassed by any in England. The juvenile performances of Miss Cooke a child three years and a half old, are very amusing. We understand the scene of St. George and the Dragon is very good.[2]"

The troupe then moved on to Great Yarmouth, Norfolk's largest town. The first performance was on 26 March and the amphitheatre was sold out. Indeed, on Monday 31 March an accident had occurred during the performance, because the audience was so large:

"Mr. Cooke, who is now on his first visit to Yarmouth has been fortunate enough to secure a site for the erection of a commodious and convenient building on Theatre Plain. The performances commenced most auspiciously on Wednesday se'nnight, and we doubt not that the visit he has paid us, while it affords abundant gratification to those who attend, will prove encouraging to the spirited and worthy proprietor. Mr. Cooke has provided not only a spacious amphitheatre, but a phalanx of artists, (about fifty in number) with a stud of thirty horses. The performances are most attractive. Those of Messrs. Cooke and Barlow, in various characters they sustain, are unrivalled; while the chastity of the comicalities introduced are inoffensive to the most fastidious taste. The house has been filled to overflowing every evening; and we should imagine that the attendance each night has not been less than 12 to 14 hundred. Mr. C's stay will be short, and we recommend to all lovers of equestrian, gymnastic, and pantomimic performances, to pay him an early visit. We observe tomorrow evening [Friday] Mr. Cooke intends giving the proceeds of the entertainment to the Yarmouth Hospital, when we hope to see a good attendance.

"Accident — On Monday evening last, an accident occurred at Cooke's Circus, in the 2nd act of 'St George and the Dragon,' in consequence of the gallery being so crowded that a number of persons ventured themselves on the boarding thrown over the avenue leading to the stables; this not being sufficiently strong to bear so great a weight, broke down with a tremendous crash. We are happy to say, that only one person was seriously injured, a man named William Lilly, aged 53, who had his leg broken in two places. Mr. Cooke immediately sent for a fly, which conveyed him to the Hospital, and we are happy to state that he is, under the hands of Mr. F. Palmer, doing well.[3]"

By the last week of April, audiences at the circus had not dwindled and the arrival of William's brother, Alfred, made them as strong as ever.

"Cooke's Circus — This most agreeable and interesting scene of amusement has presented a fund of attraction during the past week, which may be fairly pronounced unrivalled, and we are glad to find Mr. Cooke has not catered unsuccessfully. The circus, which is by far the most capacious ever erected in this town, has been crammed almost to suffocation; and the performances themselves have been highly creditable to the performers themselves and to Mr. Cooke. The exquisite skill and taste of Mr. G. Cooke and Master W. Barlow, in a new comic act (on two coursers), entitled 'The Toad in a Hole, or a Christmas Pie,' received great applause; as also did the performance of 'Dog Nelson,' and Signor Germani, the Italian Juggler. — On Wednesday evening, Mr Alfred Cooke made his first appearance in this town (having just arrived from Manchester with his stud of horses, previous to the company going to London). Being the first sight of 'Turpin's Ride to York, or the Death of Black Bess,' the arena was crowded to excess, and Mr. A. Cooke was warmly cheered at the close of the performance.[4]"

By May 1845, Nelson had performed his stunt with the geese and washing tub dozens of times and there was no reason why he should not do so in Yarmouth with his benefit night scheduled for Friday 2 May.

Nelson followed the usual routine issuing both posters and handbills, which drew on his previous exhibitions and made reference to the other 'Nelson' and local hero[5].

"This Feat had been performed by Mr. Nelson, not only at Aberdeen, Glasgow, Perth, Falkirk and the Islands of Jersey and Guernsey last, also on The broad waters of the German Ocean and on the River Thames on Monday October 11, 1844 for a wager of 60 guineas. The only successful trainer of Geese.

"The Public are particularly requested to observe that the "gallant barque" in which this singular voyage is to the accomplished is but a Common Washing Tub, only 10 inches deep. The signal for Starting will be the discharging of a GUN from the deck (rim) of Nelson's Vessel (tub) 'The Victory'."

The plan was that Nelson would set off from Yarmouth Bridge at five thirty in the afternoon and, helped by the tide, 'sail' up the River Yare and into the Bure, finally alighting at the Vauxhall Gardens next to the suspension bridge.

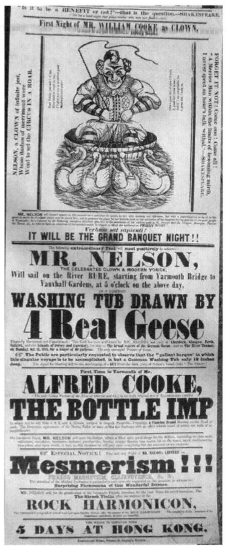

PLAYBILL ADVERTISING NELSON'S BENEFIT AT COOKE'S ROYAL CIRCUS, MAY 2ND 1845

Yet everything did not proceed as planned, for strong currents drew the tub, and the boat pulling it by a weighted rope, further than expected up

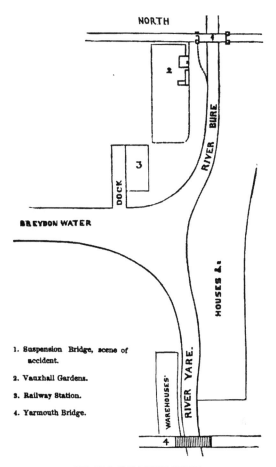

PLAN OF THE SITE
Illustrated London News 10 May 1845, p.298.

the Yare and into the mouth of Breydon Water. The delay heightened the expectation and excitement of the crowd in their hundreds lining both sides of the river. In excess of 400 had gathered on the suspension bridge jostling for the best view. On hearing the shout, "Here come the geese", they moved to the south side of the bridge en masse[6]. One observer later commented, "the bridge once convex roadway had flattened". With hardly a warning, the excited crowd was projected into the river as one side of the south suspending chain gave way.

Many horrific and heroic tales were told of the next few seconds and minutes as men, women and children became an entangled mass with

FALL OF THE SUSPENSION BRIDGE, GREAT YARMOUTH ON
FRIDAY 2ND
Illustrated London News 10 May 1845, p.289.

wood and chain. "One man fell across a piece of iron with his head just above the water, he reached to two girls who were struggling for life, and a third caught hold of his collar. All four were saved". "Eliza, the daughter of Mr James Borking, a dyer, aged 12 whose sister was drowned survived when she got hold of a man's leg and pulled her out." While the son of Mr Jay, the baker in White Lion Gates, said that when he was under the water, the people looked as if they were hugging each other. "He could see them quite perfectly."

The Illustrated London News reported that:

"Those who witnessed it asserted that not a scream was heard, nor a sound emitted from the unfortunate victims. A fearful splash and a few gurgling struggles, only recognised the spot which had swallowed such a mass of human life. Some few men hanging by the broken chains were earnestly entreated to maintain their hold, but it was soon observed that, in consequence of the obstruction of the stream by the fallen bridge, and the human bodies below, that the advancing tide would soon bury them even from sight. Every boat was immediately in requisition, and as many as twenty-five were soon on the spot, and rendered active and gallant service. The scene at this moment beggars description – husbands and wives, parents and children, were excited with the deepest anxiety. The efforts to save the victims were noble and praiseworthy. ...

"The various incidents of the tragic scene are some of them very touching. The children, many of them found with their heads fast in the railings (which on bursting the chains, lapped over into the water), doubtless fixed in that position in their anxiety to feast their eyes on the expectant sight. It was with difficulty that they were extricated, and there were some discovered with their heads smashed to pieces by the falling iron-work.[7]"

The following year, Charles Barber in his guide book for visitors to the town, summed up the catastrophe:

"Some buffoonery was being practised upon the Bure, or North river, by a clown of an equestrian troop, near that part then crossed by a Suspension Bridge, whose piers and broken chains still stand as melancholy monuments of the scenes of that fatal day ...

"Who shall describe the fearful impression upon the minds of the spectators from the shore. Who shall paint the various passions and emotions which exhibited themselves in their countenances! Who shall tell of the anxiety of mothers who looked for their offspring — of husbands who sought their wives — of wives who cast a wild look of enquiry for their husbands — of brothers, sisters, and friends, who sought those who were dear to them, to be assured that they were not among the number engulphed!

"What pen, what pencil, could convey a sufficient idea of the fearful tumult that ensued in the endeavour to escape the gurgling waters, and in the efforts of the bystanders to save the drowning! Those who witnessed that fearful scene will never become forgetful of its features — those who saw it not, can never fully feel its horrors. Many were rescued, and many were restored from almost the gates of death — and yet seventy-nine out of the number of those who went out to witness the mummery, never told its tale![8]"

On the morning after the collapse of the bridge, William Cooke appeared in front of the magistrates of the town:

THE REMOVAL OF THE SUSPENSION BRIDGE ON MONDAY
5 MAY 1845
Illustrated London News 10 May 1845, p.298.

"TOWN HALL — Saturday Morning Ten o'clock.

"The Magistrates met at this hour; there was a very full bench The Mayor, W. H. Palmer, Esq, in the chair.

"Mr. W. Cooke, the proprietor of the Circus, (who appeared to be labouring under great mental excitement,) proceeded to address the bench. He informed the Magistrates that he had come to the conclusion of withdrawing the company from the town.⁹"

That evening he distributed the following handbill in the town:

"It is with the deepest feelings of regret that Mr. W. Cooke has to announce to the gentry and inhabitants of Yarmouth, his intention of immediately closing his Circus, in consequence of the melancholy circumstance which has so recently occurred. No person can feel more deeply than he does the sad catastrophe which has filled with grief the inhabitants of Yarmouth. He trusts a discerning public will trace the

MEMORIAL TO THE VICTIMS OF THE GREAT YARMOUTH SUSPENSION BRIDGE DISASTER, ERECTED 28 SEPTEMBER 2013

calamity to its proper source – the Bridge, not being of sufficient strength to support the weight of so many persons; as the circumstance might have occurred in witnessing any public exhibition.[10]"

William Cooke was not the only one distressed by the catastrophe. The Times reporter, sent to the town, tells us on Wednesday 7 May:

"It is generally stated that Nelson, the Clown, the unhappy yet innocent cause of this sad catastrophe, has been very deeply affected by the consequences of the foolish exhibition in which he took so prominent a part, and that he has suffered great mental and bodily anguish. He left Yarmouth last night.[11]"

Some however blamed Nelson and considered that he should never undertake the exhibition again[12].

"… never have we recorded so dire an event in a locality, proceeding from so trivial, so foolish a cause, as far as human actions can be considered the causes of unfathomable dispensations of Providence. The silly exhibition of a buffoon endeavouring to symbolise the very lowest degree of intellectual vagary, by the device of four geese drawing one — in the name and form so far as his mumming attire allowed a man — for the amusement of a gazing multitude — so childish an exhibition as that has been the immediate occasion of filling a whole town with grief and hurrying into the presence of their maker above one hundred immortal souls![13]"

The evidence shows that it was some two and a half years before he undertook it a further time[14].

The number of recorded occasions that Nelson undertook the stunt diminished over the years, but this did not stop the popularity of the spectacle wherever and whoever performed it. Some two months before Nelson reprised his stunt, another accident occurred in Sheffield where Harvey Teasdale, the clown at the visiting circus, decided to perform the 'trick' using four ducks on the River Dun:

"The Love for Novelties. — We last week noticed the announcement by a comedian, named Teasdale, of a performance at the circus, under the title of 'The Chesterfield Murder.' The authorities having very properly prevented the carrying out of Mr. Teasdale's intention, it appears he was not to be disappointed in his wish to treat the public to some novelty. Accordingly he announced that, on the evening of Monday last, he would be drawn in a tub, by four ducks, from the Iron bridge to the Lady's bridge. Mr. Teasdale was not disappointed in what he anticipated would be the effect of this announcement. At the appointed time, thousands of persons, male and female, thronged the bridges, banks, and avenues leading to the river to witness the performance of this feat. Mr. Teasdale, who is a clown at the circus, started with his tub and ducks from the Iron bridge. Both were, however, perfectly unmanageable. The ducks would not go as directed by him, and the tub, after rocking for some time from side to side, overwhelmed, and turned its occupant, amidst the laughter of the lookers on, into the water. All were anxious on both margins of the river Dun to witness the various mishaps which Teasdale met with; and it was truly laughable to see him pushing his boat and ducks forward, in shallow water, towards the Lady's bridge, his intended landing place. At this juncture, the scene was changed from merriment to disaster, as about twenty yards of a wall fell in a yard in the Wicker, laden with spectators, including four or five females, and nearly thirty were precipitated into the water beneath, a depth of at least ten feet from the yard. Fortunately, it was not deep enough to drown any of them, but several met with severe bruise and contusions, and were not released without considerable difficulty. In a yard, at the tilt, near Lady's bridge, a young man, a journeyman tailor, met with a shocking accident. There were some wooden palisadings in this place, surmounted with spikes, and he, to save his life from the rush which took place, placed both his hands upon them, and, at this moment, the rush to peep at the foolish feat was still greater, and his left hand was perforated by one of the spikes, which passed between the fore finger and went out near the wrist. One of the fingers of the other hand shared a similar fate, and it will be a miracle if he recovers the use of his right hand again. So much for 'Tomfoolery.'[15]"

In April and May 1858, the clown at Ginnett's Circus, Dan Cook, performed the event three times, at Lincoln, Wisbech, where "it was estimated that not less than six thousand persons were assembled (more than half the population of Wisbech)[16]" to watch, and in Spalding where the "police were recommended not to allow the Victoria Bridge to be over crowded on Tuesday next, when Ginnett's clown would pass and down the river in a tub drawn by geese, in order to prevent any accident occurring at that Bridge.[17]"

By the late 1870s the stunt had lost its appeal and, while it was performed at the odd regatta and other events where crowds were already present, it never regained its former impact[18].

---

[1] Norfolk Chronicle — 1 February 1845, p.3. – "Cooke's Circus — Mr Cooke applied to the Mayor on Monday last, for leave to erect an amphitheatre, on the Theatre Plain, Mr. Cooke stated, that he purposed coming in about a month, and that he wished to stay five weeks. The Major granted him leave, but said he must limit the period of exhibition to a month.".

[2] Norfolk News — 18 January 1845, p.3.

[3] Ibid. 1 — 05 April 1845, p.3.

[4] Ibid. 1 — 26 April 1845, p.3.

[5] Admiral Lord Nelson landed in Yarmouth on 6 November 1800 to a hero's welcome and was given the Freedom of the Borough. At his speech from the balcony of the Wrestler's Arms he said, "I am a Norfolk man and I glory in being so!". He returned on 1 July 1801 following his victory over the Danes at the Battle of Copenhagen.

[6] Illustrated London News — May 10 1845, p.297. – This text is probably from the Norfolk News and re-used. It appears in a fuller account in the 19th issue on May 10 1845.

[7] Ibid.

[8] Barber, C. (pub) (1846) Guide to Great Yarmouth with Thirty-four Illustrations by Brooke Utting. p.39.

[9] Norfolk News — 10 May 1845, p.2.

[10] Ibid. p.3.

[11] The Times — 7 May 1845.

[12] Ibid. – "Surely, surely, it is the last time such a ridiculous, so degrading a feat, will be attempted."

[13] Bury and Norwich Post, 7 May 1845, p.3.

[14] Yorkshire Gazette — 25 September 1847, p.6. – It took place at Stockton-upon-Tees from Stockton Stone bridge down the river Tees. The event was so popular it was repeated five days later – "The banks on both sides were crowded to see this sight, and the question remains to be solved whether the people on land or the birds in the water were the greatest geese".

[15] Sheffield and Rotherham Independent — 31 July 1847, p.8.

[16] Lincolnshire Chronicle — 30 April 1858, p.3.

[17] Ibid.

[18] Edinburgh Evening News — 11 June 1877, p.4. –

"THE ACTOR, THE GEESE, AND THE TUB.

Saturday afternoon Mr. Felix Rogers, of Sanger's Amphitheatre sailed in a tub accompanied by four geese from Battersea to Westminster Bridge. The tub was two feet deep by two feet six inches in diameter, and was balanced by heavy weights, four geese being harnessed at the front. The actor was dressed in a naval captain's attire, and sat on a seat fixed across the tub. The start took place at twenty minutes to two on the ebb tide, which was flowing strong enough to carry the tub steadily along, the geese appearing to do little or nothing towards drawing it, their heads being often turned towards the actor. It was a few minutes after three when the tub passed under Westminster Bridge, and it was carried as far as a large timber wharf on the Surrey side before a landing could be effected. After some delay Mr. Rogers was got safely into a boat and rowed to the Westminster Bridge steps, where he landed amid the admiration of about 30 small children and a sprinkling of spectators on the bridge.".

5

America

Following his departure from Yarmouth, Arthur Nelson was to remain with William Cooke's Circus for its ten-week run at the New Royal Standard in Shoreditch, but there is no further mention in the press of the clown performing for the rest of 1845 with the Royal Circus or another. Certainly, by October another clown, Airdrin, had taken Nelson's place[1]. Perhaps his association with the collapse had been damaging not only to his mind and body, but also to his reputation for at the beginning of 1846, away from any limelight that might have shone on his antic, he was in New York.

Since the 18th century British performers had spent periods of time in America and vice versa, but it was in the early 19th century that it became common place. With steam-ships came cross-Atlantic performance in the 1820s, and by the 1850s came a flood of American acts and circuses to Britain and Europe. This, of course, mirrored the period of mass migration to America. The end of the Napoleonic Wars in Europe and the economic hardship that brought, coupled with industrialisation, created a class of young people who saw immigration as a way to escape the problems of unemployment at home for a better life. Demand for immigrant labour increased with two major developments: the settlement of the American Midwest after the inauguration of the Erie Canal in 1825 and the related rise of the port of New York, and the first stirrings of industrial development in the United States, predominantly textile production, in New England.

There was theatrical work to be had in the major cities of New York, Boston, Baltimore and Philadelphia and concert work in the smaller growing industrial towns. In addition, a circus tradition had developed with tented circuses visiting the small towns. While Thomas Talpin Cooke's attempt to introduce his form of circus into America in the 1830s had failed, a number of the original company stayed in The United States including his daughter Mary Ann and her husband William Cole. Mary Ann was an equestrian and performed for her father in some dramatic sequences, while William was a clown and contortionist. Their son, William Washington Cole was to form his own circus dynasty in the

United States and become a multi-millionaire[2].

During his brief time in the United States, Arthur Nelson was at no point described as a clown but seems to have confined himself to providing musical concerts, or 'musical novelties', as they were described in the advertisements placed in the local press. His first was at the Broadway Tabernacle on 14 January 1846:

"GREAT MUSICAL NOVELTY

MR. ARTHUR NELSON, the inventor of the wonderful
ROCK HARMONICON!

The most astonishing musical instrument in the world, being composed of forty simple pieces of rough stone, from the Skiddaw Mountains, Cumberland, Eng, and performed by Mr. Nelson with small wooden mallets, producing the most varied and exquisite music, unequalled by the Piano or Musical Glasses.

Also, inventor of the Musical
PINE STICKS!

Sixteen in number — on which, with wooden hammers, he performs the most difficult compositions with astonishing precision and harmony - will give

A GRAND CONCERT
On Wednesday Evening, Jan. 14th. at the
BROADWAY TABERNACLE!
Assisted by
SIGNOR BINI.
The famous Guitarist.
He will also introduce in his Concert, the
ANCIENT DULCIMER

A musical instrument celebrated in Scripture, which has been improved and perfected by Mr. Nelson, and is the only one of the kind known in the world.

The full particulars will be given in the programme of the evening. Tickets 50 cents, to be had at the door. Doors open at 6 —

The Concert to commence at 7½ o'clock, precisely.[3]"

The Broadway Tabernacle was one of the largest halls in New York, seating some 2400. Apart from services, it was also used for concerts and rallies. Built in 1836, it was considered one of the most influential churches in America and in the late 1830s was under the leadership of Charles Finney who was known for his anti-slavery rhetoric and writings.

BROADWAY TABERNACLE 1845
The Miriam and Ira D. Wallach Division of Art, Prints and
Photographs: Print Collection, The New York Public Library.

Within a week, Nelson had moved to Barnum's American Museum on the corner of Broadway and Ann Street[4]. Opened in 1842, and a forerunner of Barnum's famous circus, it is seen as central to the development of American popular culture:

"Barnum filled the American Museum with a stupefying surfeit of exhibits and activities: dioramas, panoramas, 'cosmoramas,' scientific instruments, modern appliances, a flea circus, a loom run by a dog, the trunk of a tree under which Jesus' disciples sat, a hat worn by Ulysses S.

Grant, an oyster bar, a rifle range, waxworks, glass blowers, taxidermists, phrenologists, pretty-baby contests, Ned the learned seal, the Feejee Mermaid (a mummified monkey's torso with a fish's tail), a menagerie of exotic animals that included beluga whales in an aquarium, giants, midgets, Chang and Eng the Siamese twins, Grizzly Adams's trained bears and performances ranging from magicians, ventriloquists and blackface minstrels to adaptations of biblical tales and 'Uncle Tom's Cabin.' Some 38 million customers paid the 25 cents admission to attend the museum between 1841 and 1865. The total population of the United States in 1860 was under 32 million.[5]"

THE FIRST BARNUM MUSEUM, NEW YORK
The New York Clipper Annual 1892, p.23.

While American theatrical and circus performance at first imitated that in Britain, which therefore helped performers to make the transition, it also had its unique characteristics. It was perhaps at Barnum's American Museum that Nelson came into contact with these differences as he appeared with a number of home-grown acts and artistes:

"AMERICAN MUSEUM —Every day and evening this week, commencing Monday, Jan. 19 — Splendid Performances every evening at

7 ½ and Wednesday and Saturday afternoons at 3 o'clock. — The manager has engaged Mr. Arthur Nelson, inventor of the Rock Harmonicon; Musical Pine Sticks, also performer on the Ancient Dulcimer, celebrated in the history of the Psalmist David. Also, the original Kentucky Minstrels. Also, Italian Fantoccioi, The Dissolving Views and Chromatrope. Also, Messrs. J. R. Hall, Harrison, Miss de Merlin, Billy Whitlock, Madame Rockwell, the fortune teller.
Admission 25 cents. Children under 10, 12½ cents.[6]"

For example, Billy Whitlock was a popular blackface[7] minstrel singer who, at this time, was also a member of the Kentucky Minstrels with T. G. Booth, John Hodges (Cool White), and Barney Williams.

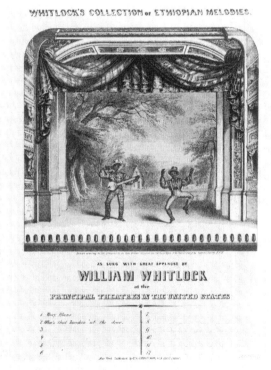

WHITLOCK'S COLLECTION OF ETHIOPIAN MELODIES AS SUNG WITH GREAT APPLAUSE BY WILLIAM WHITLOCK AT THE PRINCIPAL THEATRES IN THE UNITED STATES.
Library of Congress Prints and Photographs Division.

Nelson could well have encountered blackface minstrel singers in Britain since Billy Whitlock, Dan Emmett, Richard Pelham and Frank Brower, calling themselves the 'Virginia minstrels'[8] had come to Britain in 1843[9]. Their first engagement on arriving in Liverpool was at the Music Hall in Bold Street:

"THE FOUR VIRGINIA MINSTRELS FROM AMERICA

In a GRAND VOCAL and INSTRUMENTAL ETHIOPIAN CONCERT, at the Music Hall, Bold-street, This Day, (Friday) and 2nd, To-morrow, (Saturday) the 3rd, and Monday next, the 5th instant, when they will delineate, through the medium of new and original Negro Melodies, Lectures and Dances, the SPORTS and PASTIMES of the SLAVE RACE of AMERICA.[10]"

Whitlock had a long-necked, four-stringed banjo, which he played by striking the strings with his fingernail. He also did a 'Locomotive Lecture' in which he feigned a complete lack of knowledge about steam engines and the railway. Dan Emmett played the fiddle while Richard Pelham played the tambourine as well as being a renowned dancer. Richard Brower played the 'bones'[11] and earned a reputation as a first rate dancer introducing acrobatic leaps to the stage which caught on with other blackface performers.

Their next stop was Manchester where the Manchester Times said of their performance:

"THE VIRGINIA MINSTRELS. — This novel 'importation' of Virginia minstrels has this week been gratifying the inhabitants of Manchester with exhibitions uniting the song and dance, illustrative of the social and festive habits of the sable sons and daughters of the slave states of America. The minstrels are four in number, and are admirably dressed for their respective parts. They accompany their songs and jigs with the banjo (a rude guitar), the tambourine, fiddle, and castanets formed of bones. Their performances consist of three parts, and comprise songs, refrains, quizzical lectures, and dances. As may be expected, there is not much harmony in the airs, but there is plenty of American drollery in the words of the songs. As specimens of the festive enjoyment of the negroes of America, all the performances are highly interesting, and their novelty adds particularly to the attraction, as hitherto, with the exception of

Rice's[12] illustrations, the English people have not been favoured with any genuine display of Ethiopian life. The parody called the 'Fine old coloured gentleman' (the air being the celebrated English one), and 'Miss Lucy Long,' are the favourite melodies, and they, of course, are received with boisterous applause. The dances are singularly attractive, and are really well performed. The first is, the Slave Match Dance, as performed during the holidays in the southern states by the male slaves, in the presence of their master overseers and other whites, who urge the negroes to their utmost skill by making small presents to the negro who can stand the most fatigue or remain upon the board for the longest time. The second is the celebrated Slave Marriage Dance, as performed by the most expert dancer on the plantation, he being held in high favour by the rest of the slaves for his skill in the heel and toe science. The third is the Corn Husking Jig, in which the most expert dancer is selected. After the gathering in of the corn crop, and whilst both male and female slaves are being employed in husking corn, he amuses them by his antics and grimaces to the music of the banjo, as played by some worn-out slave, whose age alone prevents him from joining in more arduous work. It will be seen by advertisement that the minstrels perform this evening, at the Athenaeum.[13]"

When they got to London, the Era was less complimentary of their performance at the Adelphi:

"To be sure the present partie quarré smack more of New York than ould Virginy, though the dialect is capital, the action true, and the laugh unexceptionable. The gentleman who assists with the slate castanets, is vigorous, humorous, and artistic. The banjoist, though not equal in grace and execution to Sweeny[14], is a regular swinge cat[15], and the white-headed violinist is an out-and-out Rosin-the-Bow[16]. Their selection is good, but might be better.[17]"

Also on the bill at the American Museum, was William B. Harrison, a comic singer from Lambeth, London who had emigrated to America in 1841. Nelson and Harrison were to complement each other over the next few weeks in order to entertain audiences with 'musical novelty' concerts in Boston and Lowell, Massachusetts[18]. Harrison specialised in improvised singing as one review of his performance with Nelson explains:

hed in by
persons in the audience, was funny enough. The subjects, as nearly as we
can remember, were, hope, phrenology, mesmerism, affection, and several
others, the last of which was 'persons present.' On this latter subject he
sang we should say something like forty stanzas, in which he 'took off,' as
he termed it, the appearance, &c., of almost that number of persons in
the audience. One lady was described as looking through her opera glass;
such a gentleman was leaning on his umbrella; another 'had gone to sleep,
no he hadn't, he only closed his eyes to hear better.' These allusions were
all made so pleasantly, that no one could be offended at them, and as the
audience invariably turned to see the one indicated, it created much
amusement.

"'I hope you won't think it raillery,
If I tell the young man in the gallery,
That although at him I will not scoff,
Before the ladies his hat should be off—'

"is something like a part of some 'advice' he gave to a young gentleman,
who was, perhaps, not perfectly familiar with concert etiquette.[19]"

From the published programmes in Boston, one can get a clear sense of
the evening's entertainment, in which Nelson plays popular tunes that
would be familiar to audiences on both sides of the Atlantic including
those that were distinctly American in nature, such as Dandy Jim of
Caroline[20] and Yankee Doodle:

"CONCERTS IN BOSTON.
January 29.

MESSRS. NELSON AND HARRISON.

Away to the Mountain's Brow, Bid me discourse, The Arab Steed,
Overture to the Caravan Driver and his Dog: Dulcimer, by Mr. Nelson.

Comic song, by Mr. Harrison.

A fall in the frozen river, Russian quickstep, I have plucked the fairest
flower, Dandy Jim of Caroline : Rock Harmonican, by Mr. Nelson.

Comic song, by Mr. Harrison.

La Payson et Matelol, quick steps: Musical Sticks, by Mr. Nelson.

Comic song, by Mr. Harrison.

Jenny Jones, with variations, Let fame sound the trumpet: Dulcimer, by Mr. Nelson.

Song, by Mr. Harrison, extempore, upon subjects written upon cards by persons in the audience.

Blue bells of Scotland, Star Spangled Banner, Yankee Doodle: Rock Harmonican, by Mr. Nelson.[21]"

Harrison returned to Barnum's Museum and became the manager for Lavinia Warren, a proportionate dwarf, from her first appearance until she married General Tom Thumb (Charles S. Stratton) in February 1863. He then exhibited Minnie Warren, her sister, with Commodore Nutt, before joining the Ellinger and Foote Combination, a troupe of rival proportionate dwarves made up of Commodore Foote (Charles W. Nestel), his sister Eliza Nestel and Colonel Small (Joseph Huntler), who

GEN. TOM THUMB, MISS LAVINIA WARREN, COMMODORE NUTT AND THE GIANT (WILLIAM B. HARRISON)
Library of Congress Prints and Photographs Division.

toured the United States and Canada. Their advertisements often goaded P. T. Barnum by challenging him and the world to produce smaller people[22].

Barnum had first brought Charles Stratton to Britain in 1844 where, on his departure, one New York paper described the scene:

"Not less than ten thousand person joined in procession yesterday, to escort this wonderful little man on board the ship Yorkshire, by which splendid packet he sailed, in company with his parents and Mr. Barnum, proprietor of the American Museum, for the purpose of visiting her Majesty the Queen Victoria and the nobility of England. The procession passed down Fulton-street, preceded by a brass band. The General was in an open barouche, and bowed very gracefully to the thousands of ladies who filled the windows, on each side of the street, and who testified their delight at seeing him by the waving of thousands of white handkerchiefs. The shipping adjacent to the Yorkshire was black with the multitude gathered to witness the departure of the smallest man and finest ship that the world ever produced. Our little countryman will astonish the citizens of the old world.[23]"

Barnum introduced him at the Princess Theatre:

"The curtain had descended upon 'Don Pasquale;' the orchestra remained inactive; the audience was mute; the bell tinkles; the gorgeous drop-scene rises, and from the wings enters — a long, lank gentleman, agile enough seemingly for a hunter of indigenous Indians, and looking as hungry as a cannibal; this personage was Mr. Barnum, the respected proprietor of the Museum at New York, who obligingly intimated that his little friend, the General, would, with the permission of those he saw around him, make his first bow to the British public. No sooner said than done: far up the stage,

"'Tis distance lends enchantment to the view;'

"emerging through a door, a little dark speck is visible; but it progresses more rapidly than the cloud strained at by the eager vision of Sister Anne, in the ever-memorable melo-drama of 'Blue Beard;' pitter-patter, an infant that has by some magic process, jumped out of its cradle, and abjured its pap for popularity, advances towards the stage lights; can it speak as well as walk; aye, and sing too in notes both laudable that:

'Yankee Doodle came to town
Upon a little pony,
With a feather in his cap –
Oh! What a macaroni.'

"Language positively fails in depicting the thrill and wonder, blent with admiration, that ran through the house; public favor was almost fearful to give way to its wonted uproarious outburst, for fear of puffing from the face of the stage the pigmy specimen of humanity; … The hero of the evening was called before the curtain at the close of his performance; when greeted with enthusiastic shouts from all quarters, he bowed his acknowledgments in the most graceful and collected manner.[24]"

There would seem to be a symbiotic relationship between British and American popular culture and performance starting in the 1840s that might be described as the beginnings of Americanisation in Britain. The assimilation of many traditional English, Scottish and Irish songs can be quoted as an example of nineteenth-century Americans consuming, appropriating and then naturalising symbols and institutions that were, in origin at least, British. With mass emigration to America beginning in earnest in the 1830s and 1840s, it is not surprising that popular culture was also imported. This helped to ensure that performers, such as Arthur Nelson, could work both sides of the Atlantic. That said, it is noted that in America, Nelson seems to have dropped his clown persona concentrating on his musical talents and leaving it to others more practiced in the comic tastes of the American audiences. Indeed, a number of his contemporaries did not have the advantage of the neutrality of music. Nineteenth century white Americans could be ambiguous and changeable in their attitude towards England and the English in particular. Tom Barry, the clown that worked with Nelson at Astley's during the mid-1840s did not fare so well towards the end of the decade when he visited America in 1849:

"TOM BARRY, THE CLOWN, having returned from his visit to Brother Jonathan[25], has re-engaged with Mr. Batty, of the Royal Amphitheatre, and will make his first appearance on Monday next. Either the Yankees did not like Tom Barry, or Tom Barry did not like him; certain it is the facetious dispenser of broad grins has returned sooner than was anticipated, and with no amiable feelings towards 'Uncle Sam.' He is sure however, of a hearty welcome in his old quarters.[26]"

However, the British also absorbed anything new that came across from America and were soon integrating blackface minstrel melodies and songs into their own forms of entertainment. A striking example is the pantomime that Barry performed in almost immediately on his return in the winter of 1849/50. It was perhaps inevitable that Nelson Lee, the most prolific of the period's pantomime writers was to produce, 'Yankee Doodle comes to Town upon his Little Pony; or, Harlequin, how many Horses has your Father got in his Stable?', described in the playbills as a 'new and entirely original transatlantic and Britannic libretto'. The Morning Chronicle further remarked, "and the bills are strictly correct, for as far as we remember this is the first time of Yankee Doodle being impersonated in close relation with Sam Slick, Lucy Long and other characters in nigger song and our own Britannia.[27]" Lee's confidence in using these characters shows perhaps how well recognised they would have been to the audience he was writing for.

Lee was not the only one to exploit the growing cachet of America in Britain. In January 1850, the advertisement for Nelson's pantomime engagement at the Royal Victoria Theatre mentions his "wonderful performance on the Ancient Dulcimer, American Pine Sticks, and Rock Harmonicon, forms the greatest attraction and novelty in London.[28]" By June, he is described as "the American Harmonist, on the Pine Sticks and Niagara Stones[29]".

Finally, in the 1850s circuses in Britain had to compete with an influx of American tenting circuses. During this period, Nelson had engagements with Hernandez, Stone and Newcome's American Equestrian Establishment, Bell's American Circus and Howes' and Cushing's American Circus among others. On many occasions, in the marketing for these establishments he was described as an 'American clown'.

---

[1] Worcester Herald — 18 October 1845, p.2. – "Rival clowns, Messrs. Swan and Airdrin."

[2] Stout, W. L. (2002) Chilly Billy, The Evolution of a Circus Millionaire.

[3] Morning Courier and New York Enquirer — Jan 1846.

[4] New York Evening Mirror — 19 January 1846 – "American Museum — Mr. Nelson whose extraordinary performance on the Rock Harmonicon, sticks, and Dulcimer excited so much surprise at the Tabernacle last week, is engaged here, and makes his appearance to-night, The usual variety of evening performances are likewise given."

[5] Strausbaugh J. (2007) When Barnum Took Manhattan, New York Times website – http://www.nytimes.com/2007/11/09/arts/09expl.html (last accessed 22 May 2015).

[6] New York Tribune — January 1846.

[7] 'Blackface' is a form of theatrical makeup used by performers to represent a black person. The practice gained popularity during the 19th century and by 1848, blackface minstrel shows were an American artform in their own right.

[8] The Virginia Minstrels were the first group of blackface minstrels to perform a full minstrel show at the New York Bowery Amphitheatre on 6 February 1843.

[9] The first 'minstrel show' in Britain was on 8 March 1841 in Bristol according to the Juba Project which documents evidence and sources of blackface ministrelsy in Britain, — https://minstrels.library.utoronto.ca/ (last accessed 26 May 2015).

[10] Liverpool Mercury — 2 June 1843, p.1.

[11] Two animal rib bones about 20cm (9 inches) in length which when separated by a finger are played like castanets or spoons.

[12] Thomas Dartmouth Rice, the 'father of American minstrelsy', performed a song-and-dance routine in blackface and tattered clothes. Rice's character was based on a folk trickster called Jim Crow that was long popular among black slaves. Rice also adapted a traditional slave song called 'Jump Jim Crow'. In 1836 he popularised blackface entertainment with English audiences when he appeared in London.

[13] Manchester Times — 10 June 1843, p.4.

[14] Joel Sweeney was another early blackface minstrel who played the banjo and reputedly added a fifth string to the instrument. He was often the benchmark by which other banjo players were compared. He also toured Britain and Europe in 1843.

[15] A fiery or violent tempered person — McLeod Mathews, M. (1930) "Southern Backwoods Diction 1829-1840, PhD Thesis University of Chicago p.212. https://library.indstate.edu/about/units/rbsc/mss/PDFs/ mathews_diss_1930.pdf (last accessed 22 May 2015).

[16] An 1838 American folk song in which the singer relates life to playing a violin. Rosin the Bow

I've always been cheerful and easy,
And scarce have I needed a foe.
While some after money run crazy,
I merrily Rosin'd the Bow.

Some youngsters were panting for fashions,
Some new kick seemed now all the go,
But having no turbulent passions,
My motto was "Rosin the Bow."

So kindly my parents besought me,
No longer a roving to go,
And friends whom I thought had forgot me,
With gladness met Rosin the Bow.

My young day I spent all in roving,
But never was vicious, no, no;
But somehow I loved to keep moving,
And cheerfully Rosin'd the Bow.

In country or city, no matter,
Too often I never could go,
My presence all sadness would scatter,
So cheerful was Rosin the Bow.

The old people always grew merry,
Young faces with pleasure did glow,
While lips with the red of cherry,
Sipped "bliss to old Rosin the Bow."

While sweetly I played on my viol,
In measures so soft and so slow,
Old Time stopped the shade on the dial,
To listen to Rosin the Bow.

And peacefully now I am sinking,
From all this sweet world can bestow,
But Heaven's kind mercy I'm thinking,
Provides for old Rosin the Bow.

Now soon some still Sunday morning,
The first thing the neighbours will know,
Their ears will be met with the warning,
To bury old Rosin the Bow.

My friends will then so neatly dress me,
In linen as white as the snow,
And in my new coffin they'll press me,
And whisper "poor Rosin the Bow."

Then lone with my head on the pillow,
In peace I'll be sleeping below,
The grass and the breeze shaken willow,
That waves over Rosin the Bow.

[17] The Era — 25 June 1843, p.5.

[18] Nelson and Harrison performed at the Mechanics' Hall in Lowell, a mill town, called the 'American Manchester' by Alexander Mackay in 1846, and some twenty-five miles from Boston. — "Every attention is also paid in Lowell to the education, not only of the young, but also of the adults. By economy of their time and means the women not only manage to be instructed in the elementary branches of education, but also to be taught some of the accomplishments of their sex. It would not be easy to find a more acute and intelligent set of men anywhere than are the artizans and mechanics of Lowell. They have established an institution for their mutual improvement, which is accommodated in a substantial and handsome-looking edifice known as Mechanics' Hall." — Mackay, A. (1847) The Western World Travels In The United States In 1846-1847 – http://library.uml.edu/clh/All/mac.htm (last accessed 26 May 2015).

[19] Johnson, A.N. and Johnson J. jun. (1846) —The Boston Musical Gazette. Volume 1—1846.

[20] This tune comes from the American minstrel tradition being published in 1843 with the first stage adaptation being made by Dan Emmett. By the time Nelson went to America, the song was already known, appearing in a songbook by Henry Russell in 1846. In January 1846, Henry Philips sang it at the Music Hall in Dublin — "he [Henry Philips] made his bow before a Dublin audience on Friday evening, in a monologue entitled, 'Recollections of America,' interspersed with songs, which he repeated again last night. This entertainment consists of a recital of the adventures and scenes he encountered from the moment of his departure from Great Britain to his arrival in America, and throughout his wandering in the States. The prose portion of the monologue is unpretending and occasionally very amusing, and was delivered with proper emphasis and effect by Mr. Philips. In the songs, his noble manly base voice, in its full prime, told with powerful effect, and won the warmest plaudits of the audience. They are almost all original, and composed by Mr. Philips himself. The nigger songs which he gave were quite a different style from that in which we have been accustomed to hear them, and to our taste (from the enthusiasm of the audience we judged to theirs also), much more agreeable and effective. 'Old Dan Tucker' and 'Dandy Jim of Caroline,' were hailed with rapturous applause. To-night is the last of his engagement, we understand it cannot possibly by prolonged." – Freeman's Journal — 05 January 1846, p.2.
A copy of the sheet music for 'Dandy Jim of Caroline' by the Virginia Minstrels can be found in the Library of Congress Music collection — http://www.loc.gov/item/sm1844.391720/ (last assessed 26 May 2015).

[21] Ibid. 19.

[22] New York Clipper — 4 April 1863, p.407. — "Com. Foote and Col. Small, two of the smallest men in existence have met with great favor in their performances with Duprez & Green's Minstrels, in Canada. Although little in stature they have proved themselves the tallest kind of cards. P.T. Barnum with his characteristic modesty, advertises, that he has the smallest pair of dwarfs living, yet he does not come to time with Col. Ellinger who has repeatedly challenged him to show his pair against Ellinger's two. Col. Ellinger has now the smallest pair in the world, male and female, and when Commodore Foote starts out on his next tour through the States, and Canadas he will be accompanied by the smallest woman in the world being, by far, smaller than either of the Miss Warrens, at the far-famed Dollie Dutton."

[23] Ibid. 17. — 25 February 1844, p.6.

[24] Ibid.

[25] Brother Jonathan, when referring to Americans, was a term that probably came into use during the War of American Independence being applied by British officers to American rebels. It became the national personification and emblem of New England. By the end of the century it had almost entirely been supplanted by the term Uncle Sam (U.S.) to signify the whole of the United States.

[26] Ibid 17. — 4 November 1849, p.12.

[27] Morning Chronicle — 27 December 1849, p.6.

[28] Lloyd's Weekly Newspaper — 27 January 1850, p.6. – This is the first evidence of him being called the "Clown King", and maybe his persona in the pantomime called "Wat Tyler".

[29] Bell's Life in London and Sporting Chronicle — 9 June 1850, p.2. – It is likely that Nelson's marketing ploy to call himself an 'American' meant he also claimed his stones were from Niagara rather than Skiddaw.

6

Pleasure Gardens

The circus and theatre were not the only outlets for performers such as Arthur Nelson, and others who came from a circus background. From the restoration of the monarchy, the English pleasure garden became a fashionable place of entertainment. The city of London became defined by a social season with rounds of plays, concerts and events. Performances, whether they be dramatic, comedic or feats of daring or skill, would draw large audiences to places where people were seen and could be seen. By the middle of the eighteenth century there were more than sixty pleasure gardens within the London area, and throughout the country these were mimicked in the larger towns and cities, often being given the names of the more famous in the metropolis to add status to the establishment. These were broadly divided into three types.

The first was primarily a bowling green at pubs or tea gardens. The Vauxhall Gardens in Great Yarmouth, where Nelson was intended to land on that fateful day in 1845, was of this type. As John Preston, in his Picture of Yarmouth, published in 1819, put it:

"Besides the above first class of amusements, there are others of no ordinary attraction during the summer, and much praise is due to the proprietors of Vauxhall and Apollo Gardens, for the expence they have recently been at, in order to render these much improved places worth of patronage of the public, and where the Bowling Greens are kept in the highest order.[1]"

The second type, in the spa towns, provided gentle games and pursuits. Attractive spaces and gravelled walks were available together with a variety of entertainments and cuisine. Ladies and Gentlemen would not only partake of the waters, but also a characteristic public breakfast or supper.

The third form was that of large pleasure gardens, such as Vauxhall or Ranelagh, which offered a decadent 'fairy-tale' environment, or 'Arcadia' with fantastical sights viewed through variegated light or gilded foliage, splendid tree-lined walks with hidden vistas, statues and bandstands and 'tents' providing glimpses of exotic places such as Venice or China. One

1762 writer described Vauxhall Gardens:

"These beautiful gardens, so justly celebrated for the variety of pleasures and elegant entertainment they afford, during the spring and summer seasons, are situated on the south side of the river Thames in the parish of Lambeth about two miles from London; and are said to be the first gardens of their kind in England.

"The season for opening these gardens commences about the beginning of May, and continues till August. Every evening (Sunday excepted) they are opened at five o'clock for the reception of company.

"As you enter the great gate to which you are conducted by a short avenue from the road, you pay one shilling for admittance. The first scene that salutes the eye, is a noble gravel walk about nine hundred feet in length, planted on each side with a row of stately elm and other trees; which form a fine vista terminated by a landscape of the country, a beautiful lawn of meadow ground, and a grand gothic obelisk, all which so forcibly strikes the imagination, that a mind scarce tinctured with any sensibility of order and grandeur, cannot but feel inexpressible pleasure in viewing it. The gothic obelisk is to appearance a stately pyramid with a small ascent by a flight of steps, and its base decorated with festoons of flowers; but it is only a number of boards fastened together, and erected upright, which are covered with canvas painted in so masterly a manner, that it deceives the most discerning eye; at the corners are painted a number of slaves chained, and over them this inscription,

SPECTATOR
FASTIDIOSUS
SIBIMOLESTUS.

"Advancing a few steps within the garden, we behold to the right a quadrangle or square, which from the number of trees planted in it, is called the grove; in the middle of it, is a superb and magnificent orchestra of gothic construction curiously ornamented with carvings, niches, &c. the dome of which is surmounted with a plume of feathers, the crest of the prince of Wales. The whole edifice is of wood painted white and bloom colour. The ornaments are plaistic, a composition something like plaister of Paris, but only known to the ingenious architect who designed and built this beautiful object of admiration. In fine weather the musical entertainments are performed here by a select band of the best vocal and instrumental performers. At the upper extremity of this orchestra, a very fine organ is erected, and at the foot of it are the seats and desks for the musicians, placed in a semi-circular form, leaving a vacancy at the front for the vocal performers. The concert is opened with instrumental music at six o'clock, which having continued about half an hour, the company are entertained with a song; and in this manner several other songs are performed with sonatas or concertos between each, till the close of the entertainment which is generally about ten o'clock.

"A curious piece of machinery has of late years been exhibited on the inside of one of the hedges, situated in a hollow on the left-hand about half way up the walk already described, by drawing up a curtain is shewn a most beautiful landscape in perspective of a fine open hilly country with a miller's house and a water mill, all illuminated by concealed lights; but the principal object that strikes the eye is a cascade or water fall. The exact appearance of water is seen flowing down a declivity; and turning the wheel of the mill, it rises up in a foam at the bottom, and then glides away. This moving picture attended with the noise of the cascade has a very pleasing and surprising effect on both the eye and ear. About nine o'clock the curtain is drawn up, and at the expiration of ten or fifteen minutes let down again, and the company return to hear the remaining part of the concert; the last song is always a duet or trio, accompanied by a chorus.²"

One of the main attractions of the gardens was the fact that their informality meant that the sexes could meet freely without the normal conventions of the day:

"The following entertaining Adventure happened lately at Vaux-hall. Two young Country Gentlewomen taking the Diversions of the Place, as they walked along were whispering to each other their Complaints, that they seemed to be the only unfortunate there, all the rest of their Sex having their Humble Servants to attend them; and that nothing but the Company of two agreeable Gentlemen was wanting to make it the most delightful Spot in the World. This being overheard by two Sparks, who were under no less Concern for want of the Fair Sex, they briskly quitted their seats stept up to the Ladies, and offered their Services, which in a genteel Manner, without any Formalities, were accepted of; and after several pleasing turns in the Gardens, they mutually agreed to take Refreshment of a Bottle in one of the Arbours. During the whole time Love was the Theme, in which one of the Gentlemen shewed himself to be profoundly skilled, that he entirely gained the Affections of his Partner, a beautiful Lady of about Eighteen, and was married the next Morning. The Day after his Bride received a Letter, with Advice that her Father, a wealthy Alderman in the County of Kent, was just dead, and had left her a Fortune of 2000 l. which, with 500 l. she had at her Disposal before, made her a Prize worth any moderate young Fellows taking a trip to Vaux-Hall for.[3]"

Young ladies from the country were not the only females a man could meet there of course and the informality of the gardens made it the perfect place for prostitutes to operate, as Sir Roger de Coverley discovered in 1712:

"We were now arrived at Spring-Garden, which is exquisitely pleasant at this time of Year. When I considered the Fragrancy of the Walks and Bowers, with the Choirs of Birds that sung upon the Trees, and the loose Tribe of People that walked under their Shades, I could not but look upon the Place as a kind of Mahometan Paradise. Sir ROGER told me it put him in mind of a little Coppice by his House in the Country, which his Chaplain used to call an Aviary of Nightingales. You must understand, says the Knight, there is nothing in the World that pleases a Man in Love so much as your Nightingale. Ah, Mr. SPECTATOR! the many Moon-light Nights that I have walked by myself, and thought on the Widow by the Musek of the Nightingales! He here fetched a deep Sigh, and was falling into a Fit of musing, when a Masque, who came behind him, gave him a gentle Tap upon the Shoulder, and asked him if he would drink a Bottle of Mead with her? But the Knight, being startled at so unexpected a Familiarity, and displeased to be interrupted in his Thoughts of the Widow, told her, She was a wanton Baggage, and bid her go about her Business.

"We concluded our Walk with a Glass of Burton-Ale, and a Slice of Hung-Beef. When we had done eating our selves, the Knight called a Waiter to him, and bid him carry the remainder to the Waterman that had but one Leg. I perceived the Fellow stared upon him at the oddness of the Message, and was going to be saucy; upon which I ratified the Knight's Commands with a Peremptory Look.

"As we were going out of the Garden, my old Friend, thinking himself obliged, as a Member of the Quorum, to animadvert upon the Morals of the Place, told the Mistress of the House, who sat at the Bar, That he should be a better Customer to her Garden, if there were more Nightingales, and fewer Strumpets.[4]"

By the mid-nineteen hundreds, The Vauxhall Gardens was still a major place of entertainment although it had been struggling for some decades. Since the 1820s entertainment had become more diverse with comic songs and equestrian events side-by-side with ballet and plays. The typical entertainments by the late 1840s were similar to those found in the

PLAYBILL ADVERTISING VAN AMBURGH AND BOX JUBA
AT THE ROYAL VAUXHALL GARDENS 1848
British Library Collection BL 065796

popular theatres and concert halls and so theatrical entertainers naturally found employment in the pleasure gardens.

"The entertainments at the Gardens consisted of the feats of Professor Hemming, followed by Signor Bradbury on the corde volante. After which some elegant Floral Poses were exhibited by Signor Ricardo and his two infant children, concluding with some wonderful gymnastic feats. Next came a grand vocal and instrumental Concert, supported by the entire corps of the Gardens; in which Mr. J. W. Sharp introduced his new comic song ... The whole company of equestrians were brought into play in the Rotunda Theatre, where some beautiful acts of equitation were performed, enlivened by the drolleries of Barry, the inimitable Clown of the Ring. Mr. Pell, with his corps of Ethiopian Serenaders, and Juba, the unrivalled dancer, contributed immensely to the amusement of the visitors. Various other attractions were offered, which our space will not permit us to mention; but we must not omit the unusual brilliancy of the illuminations, which were most appropriate in their design; nor the fireworks, which were perfection.[5]"

Pell's Serenaders had appeared the previous season as John Sharp's 'The Vauxhall Comic Song-Book', published in 1847, pointed out. Indeed, the blackface minstrels had made such an impression that a song, 'Good Bye Darkies', was written to "perpetuate their fame[6]".

During 1850, the Prime Minister of Nepal, Jung Bahadur, made the first Nepalese visit to the west, being received by Queen Victoria on 19 June[7].

Jung Bahadur had undertaken a journey of several thousand miles to visit Britain on this diplomatic mission. The Nepalese had never even seen

HIS EXCELLENCY JUNG BAHADOOR, AMBASSADOR FROM THE COURT OF NEPAUL
Illustrated London News 8 June 1850, p.401.

the sea (the forbidden 'kala pani'), let alone crossed before setting out to Europe. Leaving essentially a medieval Nepal, the party were to be confronted with the glittering sophistication of London society including the delights of both Vauxhall Gardens and its rival Cremorne. As they were dazzled by the wealth and power of Victorian Britain, so the clothes and jewels worn by the exotic strangers, who enlivened the social scene in that summer of 1850, enchanted the people of London.

The outcome of the visit was that Nepal would become a reliable ally on the north eastern frontier of India and allay Nepalese fears of annexation by Britain. This was proved in 1857 when Jung Bahadur led 12,000 Nepalese troops to assist the British, and to the Gurka presence in the British army.

Nelson's performances at Vauxhall were of note and the delegation planned to visit during the grand fête to take place on 22 June:

"VAUXHALL GARDENS, – The remarkably fine weather with which June has commenced has operated favourable for the lessees of these gardens. The bill of fare is unusually attractive. Some excellent singing in the rotunda, poses plastiques in the ballet theatre, and a French troupe in the circus, fill up very successfully a tolerably long evening. The audience seems particularly pleased with Mr. Nelson, who amused them in the intervals between the feats of horsemanship with a very curious musical entertainment. First, he plays a waltz on a bundle of sticks with considerable execution and effect, and before the audience has ceased wondering at his dexterity re-appeared with a table covered with pantiles, upon which he played the 'Blue Bells of Scotland,' with most elaborate variations. Considering the materials, the effect was surprisingly melodious. The entertainment concludes with a view of the Kremlin[8], the final being a conflagration, with one of the most brilliant and beautiful displays of fireworks ever seen at Vauxhall. The 22d of this month has been fixed upon for the grand fête in aid of the Exposition of next year. The Prince of Nepaul and suite have signified their intention of being present.[9]"

It was on this occasion that Nelson received a medal from the delegation and in later years was to use the title, 'Jester to the Court of Nepaul' in advertising for work[10].

The next month, the Nepalese delegation was to return to the Vauxhall Gardens to witness the ascent of Charles Green in his Nassau balloon. The day almost ending in disaster when the balloon ditched in the River Thames near Gravesend[11]. Indeed, the competition between pleasure gardens meant that balloon ascents, in particular, were a regular and popular attraction at all of them. Apart from Charles Green, George Graham and his wife, Margaret were the most famous of these 'aeronauts'. Many of their escapades ended in disaster, and by the 1840s Mr. Graham had all but given up, leaving Mrs. Graham to describe herself as 'The Only English Female Aeronaut'.

Night ascents became the showpiece of the entertainments. For example on Friday 26 July 1850, Cremorne Gardens advertised their "EXTRAORDINARY GALA and NIGHT BALLOON ASCENT, under the immediate patronage of the Nepaulese Ambassador, who, accompanied by his distinguished brothers and suite ...[12]". While Vauxhall Gardens on the same night, advertised the first night ascent by a woman (Mrs. Graham) in which fireworks would be discharged from the balloon car[13]. Three days later, Mrs Graham and her daughters had conducted their second nighttime ascent over London in a new balloon called the 'Victoria and Albert'. A supreme publicist, Margaret Graham often provided statements to the press, who were only too willing to quote her verbatim:

"The wind blowing rather fresh at the moment of starting, a gust passing over the balloon caused a partial descent in the grounds, which was speedily remedied by discarding a small quantity of ballast, when we directly rose most majestically. Passing over Kensington-gardens, we obtained a clear bird's eye view of Cremorne, which was then illuminated, and we could distinctly hear the sounds of music ascending therefrom. The Royal Gardens, Vauxhall, my son directly looked for and pointed out, on the other side of the bridge, to his sisters. The entire view to my son and one daughter, whose first experience this was, was almost electric, and the exclamations of surprise and astonishment were equal to any I have heard emanate from persons possessed of nerve that have accompanied me; but not wishing to travel far and observing some other parks in the distance, I made ready to descend on one of them and ultimately effected this desideration at half-past eight o'clock in the centre of Richmond-park. Where, after giving the necessary directions to my son, and those persons assembled on the spot, myself and three daughters gratefully accepted the invitation of N. N. Robarts, Esq., of Besborough-park, Roehampton, and accompanied by his son, Frederick Robarts, Esq., of Hill-street, Berkeley-square (then on a visit). We proceeded to a splendid mansion at Roehampton; where, after partaking of refreshment, afforded in the true 'Old English Style,' and favoured with the kindest attentions of Mr. Robarts, his son and daughter (who were pleased to accept one of my daughter's flags), we were conducted to a brougham belonging to the family, and in it conveyed to town, attended with the most flattering encomiums and heartfelt wishes of our generous host and the members of his family then present.

"In conclusion, I cannot omit noticing the extraordinary admiration of my daughter Alice, who accompanied me on Friday night last from Vauxhall gardens, at the astonishing view London, at midnight, being the first and only attempt made by females to conduct the management of a balloon at night, and so much pleased am I with the nerve exhibited by those of my daughters who have hitherto accompanied me (four in number), that if on trial I find others of equal spirit (which I doubt not), I feel disposed (God willing) to ascend with my seven daughters at the great Exhibition of 1851.[14]"

Her luck was not to last as the following month she ascended from the Cremorne Gardens and, on landing in Booker's Fields, near Edmonton, her balloon caught fire.

"'I entered the car just after ten o'clock, at which time the wind had increased, and the gas, which during the period of inflation had been considerable expanded under the sun's rays, had by the time greatly condensed, in consequence of the heavy rain, which caused an augmentation in the weight of the netting and apparatus. The consequence was, that the balloon, which on the 29th of July, carried up five persons, would now only take myself, allowing for the weight of fireworks (75lb.), the tackle of which was not attached by the advice of Mr. Simpson, the proprietor, he fearing that if the firework came in contact with the trees they might become deranged, and cause some accident to myself. The result proved the correctness of his determination, as, with an ascending power of 80lb., I still scarcely cleared the trees. Continuing to ascend, I speedily lost trace of the metropolis,

MRS. GRAHAM'S BALLOON ON FIRE 1850
Illustrated London News 17 August 1850, p.137.

although I could distinctly hear the rolling of carriages beneath me, which continued about quarter of an hour, when the sound seemed lost in distance. I now commenced descending, which I gradually did until I heard the signal of railway train and saw some few lights; but the night being extremely dark, it was impossible to form any conjecture as to my whereabouts. I at length touched the ground, and the wind still increasing, was carried over several fields, where the grapnel took firm hold in a ditch; and for half an hour continued shouting as loud as I could for help, but to no purpose. Meanwhile, I kept the valve open to its full extent, rolling about all the while, the car at times completely turning over, and giving me plenty of trouble to retain my hold. At length, police constable 305 came over the fields to my assistance, and held on to the car. For at least twenty minutes I had no other help; but, at length additional assistance arrived, and I continued emptying the balloon. Upon walking round to see if the valve was open, a man indiscreetly came behind me with a light, which coming in contact with the escaping gas, instantaneously ignited, giving forth a volume of flame which resembled the dome of St. Paul's on fire: the effect of the sudden combustion of from 8000 to 10,000 cubic feet of gas was terrific.'

"Mrs. Graham was severely scorched on the face and hands, and part of her clothing was destroyed. The balloon was a new and beautiful one, and had been fitted up at great cost.

"We learn that a subscription has been commenced with the object of indemnifying Mrs. Graham for her loss, and books for this purpose have been opened at Messrs. Drummond's bank, Charing-cross; and Messrs. Robarts and Co., Lombard-street.[15]"

The rivalry between the Cremorne and Vauxhall became more intense when Charles Green advertised he would, at Vauxhall Gardens, emulate a stunt carried out in Paris some weeks before, when Monsieur Pontevin ascended into the sky on horseback[16]. This was counteracted by an announcement that Mr. Simpson, the director at Cremorne, had engaged M. Pontevin to repeat the stunt there. The advertisement drew the attention of The Society for the Prevention of Cruelty to Animals, who applied for an injunction to prevent him from doing so. In court, Mr. Thomas, the barrister for the society, put the argument that, "the very act of taking up a horse was in itself as act of cruelty". Mr. Green stated that not only had he conducted a similar ascent some twenty-one years before without harm to the animal, but also that his proposal was entirely different to that attempted by M. Pontevin. In Paris the horse had been suspended, "by straps from the balloon without anything to rest the animal's legs on; but in his case the animal had a strong platform under its feet, which relieved the horse from any distress occasioned by the suspension, or even the superincumbent weight of his rider, as he, Mr. Green, rested his feet on the ballast bags, and had no weight whatever on the horse's back." It then transpired, that M. Pointevin was not to appear at the Cremorne, and that the announcement "was all done to mislead the public, and annoy Messrs. Wardell and Green". Mr. Thomas added, "He could very well understand how such sights could please the thoughtless and wonder-loving people of Paris, but would think such exhibitions a disgrace to this country". The magistrate's solution was that they "substitute a wooden horse for a live animal". However, a 'veterinary gentleman' assured the court that there was no danger or cruelty to the animal and therefore the case was dismissed[17]. That evening the stunt went ahead, but the crowds were to be disappointed:

"VAUXHALL GARDENS. The equestrian aeronautic ascent which caused so great an excitement for the last few days took place yesterday. So ridiculous a termination could not have been anticipated; for, in lieu of a full-grown horse suspended to the balloon and mounted by the 'veteran Green,' the public was presented to an exceedingly small pony, standing about nine hands high, and weighing, at the outside, two hundred pounds. The little animal was gaily caparisoned, his legs secured with rope to the car, his eyes hoodwinked, and he was liberally feasted with carrots to secure his amenity. The 'ancient mariner' of the skies sat astride, his legs touching the bottom of the machine, and bags of sand were deposited therein to make all steady. The whole affair had the air of a scene in a Christmas pantomime, and seemed rather a sly burlesque upon the Frenchman Poitevin's equally absurd exhibition at Paris. The balloon shot like a rocket into the clouds, and, after a few minutes, vanished into 'thin air.' From the time that Francis Lana the Jesuit[18], in 1670, sought to support his aerial contrivance by means of four balls, to the present time — from Montgolfier to Mrs. Graham, such a ballooning folly as that of yesterday was never exhibited. The disappointment of the crowded public was vented in laughter; each man looked sheepishly at his neighbour, as though ashamed at his gullibility. The mass had come with the hope to see a poor animal tortured— they had sought an unworthy physical excitement, and verily they had their reward. All, however, terminated favourably. The pony and the veteran descended safely at Norwood, and returned to the gardens at a quarter to twelve. The pony was trotted round the illuminated arcades, amidst the cheers of the audience, and the aeronaut was complimented upon his achievement. We trust that the proper authorities will put a stop to all future exhibitions of this nature — they are worthless, cruel, and disgraceful to the country. There must have been upwards of five thousand persons assembled, and every approach to the gardens literally swarmed with people, hot with excitement to behold the equine ascent.[19]"

Cremorne Gardens in Chelsea had been established in the 1830s and, as

Vauxhall declined, it gained in reputation. In 1859, Vauxhall was closed and the land built on, while Cremorne continued to provide the sort of entertainments that Victorians enjoyed. Battle re-enactments were particularly popular and at Cremorne naval fêtes recreated famous battles from the past:

"Some men, it has been said, possess means that are great, but fritter them away in the execution of conceptions that are little, and there are others who can form great conceptions, but attempt to carry them into execution with little means. It is a rare thing to find a combination of great means and great conceptions; but, though rare, we have a striking example of their union in the director of Cremorne, whose designs are so well planned as to make it delightful to observe how effectually his means support his measures at one time, and how gratefully his measures repay his means of another. The naval fêtes, introduced at Cremorne to honour the past, to improve the present and interest the future (the fifth of which came off last night), are brilliant proof of this. Historical truth, local position, artistic taste, pyrotechnic talent – each and all were made available, by good judgment, to represent the storming of Gibraltar's renowned fort in June 1727, where the enormous Spanish force, led on by Count de la Torres, was, by his Catholic Majesty, ordered to lower the British flag, but which after repeated attempts, ended in the lowering of the Spanish one, and the abandonment of the siege, after the loss of 3000 men.

"On each former occasion the Iron and Citizen Steam-boat Company lent their boats to represent the attacking force, and were rewarded, not only by the thanks of the public, but by the more weighty consideration of heavily-laden and additional boats. On this occasion such support was not accorded, and it was feared some difficulty might arise; but the director of Cremorne, who knows no difficulty where the public are concerned, substituted canvas for steam, and when the important moment arrived a fleet of vessels appeared whose warlike aptitude prevented any disappointment. Under cover of darkness, and aided by full tide, the boats took up their moorings in a most advantageous position, and, almost before the garrison were aware of it, the first volley was fired. A few — very few moments elapsed when the governor, General Clayton (Mottram), issued orders to fire, and each gun poured forth its brilliant contents, and, as it were, compelling the assailants to retire under so hot a reception. In the course of half an hour the varied and stirring scenes of a siege were represented, the mine exploded, the brave were defeated; and when, in midst of cheers — of varied and mingled music 'God Save the Queen' appeared on the fort, the splendid red and blue lights struggling for pre-eminence admirably showed forth in vivid colours and in strong contrast the hundreds of Gibraltar's retiring enemies and the thousands of Cremorne's assembled friends.[20]"

Such extravaganzas employed the latest technology to produce the spectacle, and this was also applied to exhibitions. In 1860, Cremorne caused a sensation when it installed its Stereorama of the Pass of St. Gothard:

"THE STEREORAMA AT CREMORNE GARDENS

In addition to the already pictorial, structural, and other attractions of Cremorne Gardens, the enterprising proprietor has recently brought to

THE STEREORAMA AT CREMORNE GARDENS. — PANORAMA OF THE ROUTE TO ITALY, VIA THE ST. GOTHARD PASS
Illustrated London News 8 September 1860, p.226.

completion a novel artistic work, which he denominates the 'Stereorama.' This name is adopted on account of the attempt made to accomplish by means of painting and modelling the peculiar effects produced by the stereoscopic glasses, and more particularly the appearance of relief and solidity in objects which painting alone cannot realise. In short, it is a combination of painting for the more distant panorama with the nicest structural formation for the objects in the foreground, producing a result which so nearly approaches reality as almost to mystify the sense.

" … the spectator is in close proximity to the objects in the foreground so that he might almost pluck a leaf from a tree, or a blade of grass from the mountain path at his feet, and the highest degree of finish and exactness has therefore to be bestowed upon all that comes within this range; whilst at the same time, an eye must be kept for its general keeping with the most distance portions of the panorama. …

"When we add that real water is brought to their aid at the rate of nine hundred gallons a minute to supply the mimic torrent issuing beneath the Devil's Bridge, and thence, winding and flowing through various channels in the foreground, turning mills, &c., the reader may imagine for himself the impression upon his senses which a visit to the Stereorama is calculated to produce.

"The building in which the Stereorama is shown measures some 120 feet across, and is 50 feet high. Within this area, with a circumference of about 850 feet, and a total surface of canvas of 18,000 square feet, the immediate space being filled in with modelling work the artists represent the grandeur and more picturesque features of the stupendous scenery which presents itself to the traveller between Lake Lucerne and the Lago Maggiore; in fact, the romantic route into Italy over the Alps through the famous St. Gothard pass.[21]"

By the 1870s, the 'arcadian delight' of the pleasure gardens had all but disappeared. Forerunners of the amusement park, in the daytime the gardens had catered for families, while at night, the firework displays and rowdy behaviour, fuelled by the drinking and young men looking for the euphemistically called 'Fulham virgins', now subjugated the gentler pursuits and entertainments. The growth of the railways meant that now Victorian families wanted the latest fashion, a seaside holiday, and it was the seaside that became a replacement for the pleasure gardens. Most seaside resorts had gardens that mimicked the displays and bandstands in miniature. Many had 'winter gardens' to take tea and theatres, pier-shows, music halls and assembly rooms to cater for all tastes in entertainment.

---

[1] Preston, J. (1819) The Picture of Yarmouth: Being A Compendious History and Description of all the Public Establishments within that Borough. Available at https://books.google.co.uk/books/download/The_Picture_of_Yarmouth.pdf (last accessed 25 March 2015).

[2] Anon. (1762) A Description of VAUX-HALL GARDENS Being A proper companion and guide for all who visit that place. Available at http://www.vauxhallgardens.com/vauxhall_gardens_description_page.html (last accessed 8 June 2015).

[3] Derby Mercury — 27 July 1738, p.4.

[4] Addison, J. (1712) The Spectator No. 383 Tuesday, May 20, 1712. Available at http://www.readbookonline.net/readOnLine/40563/ (last accessed 8 June 2015).

[5] The Era — 23 July 1848, p.10.

[6] Sharp, J.W. (1847) The Vauxhall Comic Song-Book. p.215-216.— "GOOD BYE, DARKIES!
Written by F. J. Darner Cape. Arranged by Edward Clare. Published by Z. T. Purday, 45, High Holborn. The performance of the Ethiopian Serenaders—Pell, Harrington, White, Stanwood, and Germon, created during their stay in London more excitement, and aroused more interest in the public mind, than anything we recollect for many years past. They sustained their characters admirably well, and gave very correct and striking delineations of negro manners and feelings. After a most successful number of performances, they at length gave their 'Farewell Benefit,' on the 3rd of July, 1847. The above song was written, on the occasion of their taking leave, for the purpose of perpetuating their fame."

[7] Morning Post — 20 June 1850, p.5.

[8] London Standard —1 June 1850, p.2. – "The grand representation of the Kremlin at Moscow, by Mr. W. Batty, is admirably painted, and the pyrotechnic display introduces several novelties of exceeding ingenuity and brilliancy".

[9] Bell's Life in London and Sporting Chronicle — 9 June 1850, p.3.

[10] The Era —11 January 1857, p.1. – " MR. ARTHUR NELSON, Clown King and Jester Extraordinary to the Court of Nepaul, from whence he received a Gold Medal in 1851, is now concluding a starring engagement at the Theatre Royal, Dover, and will be disengaged on Monday, the 20th of January. His performances are suited to Circuses, Theatres and first-class Concert Rooms. All letters directed Refectory Tavern, Ramsgate, will be attended to. N.B. Private parties attended."

[11] Manchester Courier and Lancashire General Advertiser — 6 July 1850, p.4. – "BALLOON DISASTER – On Saturday, the Nepaulese Princes visited the Vauxhall Gardens to witness the ascent of the Nassau Balloon, which took place shortly after their arrival, and made its way through the clouds towards Gravesend, beyond which place its descent was accompanied with imminent peril to the lives of the aeronauts, as, from some cause, it descended into the river, near Jenkin buoy. A barge succeeded in rescuing Mr. Green and Mr. Rush from the balloon. The revenue cutter Fly also proceeded to the rescue, and having grappled the balloon, found it impossible to check its progress until, by discharging muskets into it, they made vents for the escape of the gas. Mr Green was very much hurt of the head and face, probably from his efforts to keep on the balloon, which was continually rolling and turning on the surface of the water."

[12] Morning Post — 26 July 1850, p.1.

[13] Ibid. – "MRS. GRAHAM'S GRAND NIGHT BALLOON ASCENT at VAUXHALL GARDENS THIS EVENING (July 26), — the first night ascent ever attempted by a female. A magnificent display of Fireworks, prepared expressly for the occasion by Darby, will be discharged from the car. … The Illuminations will be more brilliant, and the Fireworks more gorgeous."

[14] The Era — 4 August 1850, p.11.

[15] Illustrated London News — 17 August 1850, p.138.

[16] Brighton Gazette — 11 July 1850, p.8. – "All Paris is talking of an extraordinary balloon ascent which was made on Sunday afternoon in the Champs de Mars, and which it must be confessed casts the exploits of your Mr. Green and his fellows far into the shade. A man, named Pointevin, ascended on horseback. A horse was attached to the balloon in a similar way to that in which horses are hoisted on shipboard; the aeronaut, who was attired as a jockey, got on the animals back and away they went. The horse kicked a little at first, but the moment it was fairly off the ground, became perfectly tranquil. After rising to a considerable height, the aeronaut got off the animal's back and by means of a rope ladder ascended into a sort of car seven or eight feet above his head. The horse, at first, bled copiously from the mouth, but sustained no other inconvenience. After remaining in the air about an hour and three quarters, the balloon alighted in a forest in the department of Seine et Marne, near a village named Grisi, about twenty-five miles to the east of Paris."

[17] Morning Post — 31 July 1850, p.7-8.

[18] Francesco Lana de Terzi was a Jesuit mathematician who in 1670 published, an 'Essay on new inventions permitted to the master art', which contained the description of a flying ship. His design had a central mast to which a sail was attached, and four outer masts, which had thin, copper foil spheres attached to them. The air would be pumped out of the spheres, leaving a vacuum inside, so providing lift. In 1710 Gottfried William Leibniz, proved that his vacuum spheres were physically impossible to build since no one could manufacture such thin copper foil and the pressure of the surrounding air would have collapsed them.

[19] Ibid. 17. — 1 August 1850, p.5.

[20] London Standard — 21 August 1851, p.2.

[21] Illustrated London News — 8 September 1860, p.227-228.

7

Poses Plastiques and Tableaux Vivants

Among the popular entertainments of the 1840s and 1850s was that of poses plastiques and tableaux vivants. Generally described as 'living pictures', they originally differed in origin and form, but the terms became synonymous with each other during this period.

The term 'poses plastiques' was probably first used by Andrew Ducrow to describe his style of equestrian performance in the ring. In 1828 his performance was advertised as:

"MR DUCROW will repeat his last new scene, wherein he represents, upon a single horse, without quitting his saddle, seven different characters called, SEPTEM IN UNO; OR, ONE A COMPANY.[1]"

MR DUCROW IN THE VICISSITUDE OF A TAR
Billy Rose Theatre Division, The New York Public Library.

Ducrow would pose in character costume on horseback perfectly motionless, as his steed galloped around the ring. He would then take centre 'ring' to pose in recognisable classical forms, known as 'attitudes':

"Amongst a succession of other striking Equestrians in the Circle, MR DUCROW has invented, for this occasion, three New Scenes. He will appear on his rapid Courser, in a Rustic and Heroic Picture, called

ANDREW, THE MOUNTAIN SHEPHERD.
AND
ROB ROY.

This attempt, Mr Ducrow is bound to confess as complimentary to the national honour of his Friends and numerous Patrons in Edinburgh.

The Second New Classical Scene
Bears the title of
THE LIVING STATUE;
OR,
MODELS OF ANTIQUES.

Wherein will be represented by Mr. Ducrow on a pedestal in the centre of the circle, the following Portraitures:

1—6 HERCULES and the NEMEAN LION in Six Attitudes.
7, CINCINNATUS, the Roman, fastening his Sandals.
8, HERCULES throwing LYSIMACHUS into the Sea.
9, The Slave REMOULEUR (The Grinder).
10, The Beautiful Poses of the FIGHTING GLADIATOR.
11, The Group of HOMER and ANTIGONA.
12, ROMULUS, from David's Picture of the Sabines.
13, REMUS'S Defence, from the same.

This representation will conclude with Three of the positions of the
DYING GLADIATOR.²"

Ducrow would go on to train his horses to 'act' in the tableau:

"Who has not heard of the astonishing feats of this the greatest horseman who ever existed or will exist? Their tractability in this respect goes beyond anything that could be disposed. There is one beautiful white

JAQUES LOUIS DAVID – INTERVENTION OF THE
SABINE WOMEN, 1799

Two of Ducrow's poses are taken from this picture painted in 1799
which shows, Hersilia in the centre forcing herself between
Romulus, her husband, on the right, and the Sabine Tatius, her
father, on the left. It is likely that Ducrow's thirteenth pose was of
Tatius rather than Remus as Romulus's brother had died before the
event depicted in the painting.

horse, in particular, which wins all hearts. Perhaps he is the favourite of
the stud. He enters the circle in front of the stage alone, with zephyr like
wings attached to his shoulders, given to him the character of Pegasus: he
bounds or rather flies round the circle several times, as if in ecstatic
consciousness of superiority; his mane and tail erect, his fine eyes
glistening, and his open nostrils displaying a brilliant red: so sleek, so
elegant is this animal, that he is sufficient to occupy the attention of the
spectators for a time. Mr. Ducrow enters during this excitement, with
peculiar beauty of effect, as Apollo, habited in white, bearing a small harp,
delightingly classical. The sounds from the harp attract the attention of
Pegasus; he is, as it were, charmed, and becomes the gentle observer of
the wishes of Apollo. After a few caresses, Apollo mounts, and standing
on the bare back of the spirited animal commences a series of graceful
attitudes, while the harp is occasionally touched in unison with the

elegance of the performance. After twenty circuits or more, terminating with surprising fleetness of the horse and dexterity of the rider, Apollo springs on the ground; Pegasus rests himself in the centre of the circle, where a tranquil display of reclining attitudes and of beautiful groupings takes place. — Apollo and Pegasus being while, and seen under a powerful brilliancy, they appear in extraordinary lustre, altogether presenting a classical illustration of Apollo and Pegasus resting on Parnassus. This exhibition offers to the eye of taste a series of beautiful compositions, fraught with associations of a character richly poetical and highly gratifying.[3]"

Historians usually trace the origins of tableau vivant to the performances of Emma Hamilton to her friends and acquaintances at her home in Naples in the late 1700s. An accomplished actress, and having already posed for George Romney, the artist, as women from Greco-Roman mythology, she developed what she called her 'attitudes' – a cross between postures, dance, and acting. Sir William Hamilton's guests took quickly to this new form of entertainment, which took the form of a charade, with the audience guessing the names of the classical characters and scenes Emma portrayed.

Whereas Ducrow's and Hamilton's poses mimicked an individual statue or, at best, a small group within a painting, the new form of dramatic art attempted to recreate as much of the whole picture as possible. As a result many 'poseurs' were required. Certainly, in Europe theatrical performances like this were taking place as interludes or at the end of the performance. David Wilkie, the Scottish painter described in a letter of 4 July 1826:

"I have been much interested by an exhibition at one of their little Theatres, of what they call a Tableau. The curtain is drawn up between the acts, the stage darkened, and at the back is a scene resembling a picture frame, in the interior of which most brilliantly lighted from behind, men and women are arranged in appropriate dresses, to make up the composition of some known picture. One I saw the other night was an interior, after D. Teniers. It was the most beautiful reality I ever saw. Mr. Chad, the British minister, was with me. We were quite delighted with it; but so evanescent is the group, that the curtain drops in twenty seconds, the people being unable to remain for any longer period in one precise position.[4]"

That winter, while in Rome, Wilkie became more involved in tableaux, despite being rather irritated by the company:

"We have had this winter another amusement, which, by the waywardness of the chief promoter of it, has yet been more tantalizing than pleasing. The Countess of Westmoreland, of high rank and splendid establishment, but too ardent, too sensitive, and too indifferent to time, place, and the feelings of other people, has, with my friend Severn, been getting up what we called in Germany tableaux. Failures are of course inevitable; yet the night I went with Sir Robert and Lady Liston, some Tableaux with single figures, of which the subjects were very handsome women, succeeded extremely well, and one, The Sybil of Guercino, the beautiful Mrs. Cowell, was one of the loveliest visions I ever saw. But what would have attracted all Rome, was found insufficient for the great number of Lady Westmoreland's particular friends, and great offence was given by the necessary limitation of visitors, and the confusion and misrule between her Ladyship and Severn, by which some beauties, who were asked, could not, from trifling mistakes, be gratified by their appearance in the picture. In order to appease and gratify some friends, a good lady of my acquaintance asked me to try some in her house; invited some beauties on purpose, and after a few rehearsals, we got up four in the simplest manner, in a picture frame, quite as good as those of the wayward Countess. A numerous company was perfectly delighted with them, and the ladies who formed them still more so. We had The Cenci of Guido, The Sybil of Guercino, an Agrippina, and Giorgiones Gaston de Foix in armour, with the Lady placing the order on his breast. Lady Westmoreland has said she could get no one to obey her, and is asserted to have boxed Severn's ears for disobedience. I, on the contrary, found all submission: never before did I possess such an influence over sovereign beauty, or found an admired lady so manageable.[5]"

Wilkie's enthusiasm continued unabated:

"I have been busy of late directing tableaux at the Honourable Miss Mackenzie's, which have succeeded beyond our most sanguine expectations. We had, besides, Sybils and Madonnas from various pictures, various portraits: Lord Darnley, by an early master; Cardinal Bentivoglio, by Vandyke; and the finest of all, a portrait of Titian, by himself.[6]"

When Wilkie returned to England he was asked by the Duke of Wellington to produce a tableau vivant based on Walter Scott's novels for the Marchioness of Salisbury at Hatfield House in 1833. Many members of the aristocracy took part.

"GRAND FESTIVITIES AT HATFIELD HOUSE …

"The Marquis and Marchioness of Salisbury's long anticipated grand entertainment and fancy dress ball, took place on Wednesday night, at their noble mansion, at Hatfield. For some months past the fashionable modistes have been in active employ in preparing the splendid and costly costumes; since the Marchioness of Londonderry's far famed Court of Queen Elizabeth no entertainment has ever been given on so magnificent a scale, and we were even informed that the latter eclipsed the former splendid pageant. …

"Above 200 of the principal nobility were present on this splendid occasion; after a sumptuous banquet, the company proceeded to the noble saloon called the long gallery, the lower end of which was fitted up for the purpose of representing the tableau vivant. We shall proceed to notice the various dresses and characters, as they were represented by the noble guests. At ten o'clock, the room having been darkened, the curtain drew up, and presented a beautiful tableau …[7]"

While Wilkie's enthusiasm had engendered genuine interest among the upper classes for participating in such amusements, the professionalisation of tableau vivant as a stand-alone form of drama had already taken place. By 1830, Ferdinand Flor, an artist from Lübeck in Germany, had already put a troupe together, and following successes in Italy was touring Britain.

"ICONOLOGICAL EXHIBITION.

An entertainment of a very novel and pleasing description took place on Wednesday evening at the Egyptian Hall, Piccadilly. Mr. FERDINAND FLOR, an Italian Artist, whose successful performances in Rome, Naples, and Florence have induced him to visit this country, undertook to represent, by means of living persons, the Pictures of the Ancient Masters, and to present them in such a series as should convey an idea of the progress of Art and the different styles of Painting, beginning with the earliest Egyptian, and ending with the Italian and Bolognese Schools. His examples exceeded thirty in number, and it would be no easy task to describe the whole, or to do justice to the ingenuity of the design or the perfection of the execution. The living actors appeared as though they were the identical persons who were sitting for the original representations, such was the similitude or person, figure, and costume. The St. Cecilia of RAFFAELE was a most successful effort, and was marked by the plaudits or a distinguished company or upwards of two hundred persons; this and many or the other Tableaux called forth a desire for their repetition, which protracted the entertainment, and must have exhausted the performers, to whom the remaining in fixed attitudes for a length of time must have been attended with no slight inconvenience. We hail this successful attempt or Mr. FLOR at producing an entertainment which offers such variety of subjects and such means of facilitating the study or the Fine Arts. There must have been upwards or twenty persons employed, men, women, and children, and we have no doubt, when our fashionables reassemble in town, this entertainment will be a leading object of attraction.[8]"

Flor was soon invited to put on a shorter version of his entertainment in front of the Queen at Brighton[9], which led to a commission to paint her[10]. This performance was of just four tableaux between acts in the show. However, during the 1830s, the tableau vivant also became a dramatic strategy in which actors stood still within a scene of the play:

"Mr. ADDISON'S new farce of *Tam O'Shanter* followed, and occasioned a great deal of laughter. It is a sort of adaptation of the well-known poem of BURNS to the stage, and the author has done his work with much sprightly cleverness. ... In the first scene, *Tam* and *Souter Johnny* (BARTLEY) are exhibited as tableau vivant, exactly in the attitudes of Mr. THOMS' statues, and the recognition occasioned considerable satisfaction among the audience.[11]"

The integration of tableau vivants into the main action of performance meant that, not only did some performers began to perfect if not specialise in this new dramatic form, but specific theatrical considerations had to be adopted. This inevitably led to the establishment of companies of actors dedicated to this type of performance.

"The number of persons required in a first-class tableau-company is forty. It will be necessary to have that number to produce large pictures; fifteen or twenty-five persons will be sufficient for smaller representations. In forming the company, the following persons should be selected: six young ladies, of good form and features, varying in styles and sizes; six young gentlemen, of good figure, and of various heights; two small misses; two small lads; two gentlemen for stage assistants; one painter, one joiner, one lady's wardrobe assistant, one curtain attendant, one announcer.[12]"

These would have been the considerations[13] when Arthur Nelson took over the management of Madame Warton's troupe of artistes in August 1854. Madame Warton, whose real name was Eliza Crow, had appeared on the theatrical scene in October 1846 at the newly created Walhalla in Leicester Square:

"THE WALHALLA. — Late Miss LINWOOD'S GALLERY, Leicester-square. – Under the patronage of several distinguished Members of the Royal Academy. – Madame Warton begs respectfully to inform the Nobility, Gentry, and Public, that she has taken the above spacious Gallery for the purpose of carrying out, on a classic scale of splendour, the TABLEAUX VIVANS and POSES PLASTIQUES, having been favoured, during her recent visit on the Continent, with admissions to the Studios of several celebrated Sculptors and Painters, for the purpose of collecting Groupings. She has also succeeded in engaging a Troupe of eminent Artists, supported by the valuable aid of several celebrated models of the Royal Academy. They will have the honour of making their first appearance on MONDAY October 12.[14]"

By May 1847, she had introduced special coloured effects to her 'white marble groupings' with "the novel effect produced by the new Chemical Light, by Mr. G. Southby, of the Royal Surrey Zoological Gardens[15]". Which led the Era remark, "Madame Warton has been giving a series of Marble Statues (white marble, of course). We don't think they will be attended with the success that her other 'Poses Plastiques,' which have the advantage of costume, have been. We recollect many years since that similar groups of statuary were exhibited at Vauxhall, then under the management of Messrs. Gye and Hughes; they were beautifully arranged, and it strikes us, that the light thrown upon them was better managed than at the Walhalla. We should advise Madame Warton to pay attention to that adjunct, which decidedly gives the greater effect to the exhibition.[16]"

While Madame Warton's exhibitions were artistic, tableaux vivants were already acquiring a dubious reputation. The portrayal of female and male statues in 'white marble' suggested that the actors were nude, or at least scantily dressed. In reality the protagonists wore white 'fleshings' or tightly fitted body suits.

"THE WALHALLA.— When the exhibitions of tableaux vivants had become a sort of rage, we thought it our duty to point out their evil tendencies. In almost every instance the subjects introduced were suggestive of vice and obscenity. In Paris the authorities refused to grant permission for their performance. — in England the evil cured itself. That *tableaux vivants* may be made both amusing and instructive, the Walhalla sufficiently proves. Everything is here banished that may have an evil tendency — the various subjects are selected with admirable judgment, and the groupings are arranged with artistic taste. Madame Warton, the directress, and the chief model, has laboured zealously and succeeded perfectly in imparting to the various groups a truthfulness and propriety as satisfactory to the professional artist as they are delightful and instructive to the mere 'lover of fine forms' The present series of tableaux is specially interesting, as illustrating some of the most striking scenes from the plays of Shakspere. Where all is excellent, it is difficult to particularise, but we may make special mention of 'The Incantation Scene' from Macbeth, with its accompanying chorus; the Ophelia and Ariel of Madame Warton, and the scene from *Titus Andronicus*. The dresses and accessories are rich and

PLAYBILL MADAM WARTON AS LADY GODIVA, WALHALLA 1848.

appropriate, while the intermediate act music, which is performed in an admirable manner, by an excellent band, contributes to render the performances complete, and of a very elevated character.[17]"

Eliza Crow soon revealed that she was also modelling for Edwin Landseer's new painting of 'Lady Godiva's Prayer' and taking advantage of the fact by including it in her presentation:

"WALHALLA.-Madame Warton has introduced several new and picturesque groups into her programme. Among the most remarkable of these is a beautiful representation of the renowned 'Lady Godiva.' This is taken from a painting by Mr. E. Landseer, R.A., and for which Madame Warton has been for some time past sitting to the artist. The picture, when entirely finished, it is understood, is intended for exhibition during the forth- coming season, at the Royal Academy. The beautiful Lady Godiva is personated most exquisitely by the model herself, and is represented seated on the backs of her milk white steed as though riding through the streets of Coventry; the effect of the tableau is extremely graceful. This group, since its first representation, has been, on every succeeding occasion, warmly encored several times by a numerous audience.[18]"

Her tableau was so well received that it was soon heralded as her greatest achievement, and when in June it was announced[19] she would play Lady Godiva in the annual procession in Coventry[20] her reputation was assured.

Following her success in the procession, Madame Warton and her troupe began touring the provinces. Lady Godiva being her "chef-d'oeuvre" alongside Venus, Innocence, Sappho and Ariadne. The Newcastle Journal's reporter explained how the performers were clothed:

"In Madame Warton's exhibition the artistes are similarly encased in a flexible covering of silk, but the colour selected is not the chalky whiteness of stone, but that natural tint more agreeable to the eye, which nature has given to the human flesh. Appropriate drapery, arranged in classical forms, adds beauty to the figures and gives character to the picture; the expressive countenance embodying all the conceptions of the artist, exhibits a striking delineation of the prominent or conflicting passions of the moment.[21]"

Such explanation was considered necessary as by 1849 there were less tasteful versions of the art being performed. Madame Warton also found that there was another troupe touring that was playing loose with her reputation if not directly impersonating her. From April 1849, she felt it necessary to add a paragraph in her national advertisements in the Era to disassociate her troupe from the other[22]. By November, she was adding strongly worded statements to her local advertisements as well:

"MADAME WARTON takes this opportunity of informing her Patrons that she is not, nor ever has been, connected with any other Company travelling, representing themselves as connected with her ESTABLISHMENT, THE WALHALLA, LEICESTER SQUARE, LONDON, *and such, Company are wholly unauthorised and unjustified in so introducing themselves or their Establishment.*[23]"

By 1851, perhaps due to the erosion of the reputation of tableau vivants by such troupes in general, or damage being done by impersonation, Madame Warton's style of entertainment came under sustained attack. Their engagement at the Theatre Royal in Cork started badly[24], and by the end of February it became clear that they were losing the battle:

"THE Company comprising MADAME WARTON'S WALHALLA Establishment, most respectfully announce, that at the suggestion of a few friends, they intend taking a BENEFIT previous to their departure from the City (for which purpose the proprietor, A. MURRAY, has kindly granted the use of the Theatre gratuitously,) to compensate in some measure for the great loss sustained in consequence of an unfounded prejudice, and many false representations existing against the Exhibition which has been pronounced unanimously by the public Press, to be the utmost Unique and Classic Entertainment ever represented in the City of Cork.[25]"

Such views were also expressed in Dublin, where they next appeared, where Reynolds's Newspaper commented, "The Theatre Royal Dublin has been much injured through the instrumentality of Madame Warton and her *troupe* of demi-naked *figurantes*.[26]"

Only a few years before, the troupe had seen large audiences on their own account at venues like the Manchester Free Trade Hall, but was now only part of the variety of entertainments at theatres such as the Standard in Shoreditch[27].

It was at the Standard that, as far as the evidence suggests, Madame Warton and Nelson appeared on the same programme[28]. It was the start of a fruitful professional, and probably personal, relationship that was to last the next couple of years. It was also at the Standard, with its equestrian background, that Warton was able to revive her Lady Godiva persona, "on her splendid charger, as ridden by her through Coventry.[29]"

Nelson and Warton were to appear on the same bills over the next eighteen months. By January 1853, it is clear they were a complementary act:

"LEEDS. — *Theatre Royal.* — The celebrated Madame Warton and her troupe of Pose Plastiques have represented a series of pictures from the antique, with the addition of several scenes from 'Uncle Tom's Cabin,' accompanied by Mr. A. Nelson on the dulcimer. Between the entertainments Mr. Nelson, the Clown, gave his entertainment on the pine sticks and rock harmonicon, interspersed with a comic monopologue suited to the taste of all inclined to be *ridibundus*.[30]"

Some might speculate whether Nelson had a hand in the break up of the Warton's marriage. Indeed, while the troupe bore her name, 'Professor' Warton had taken the lead male roles, such as 'Mars', alongside Madame Warton's 'Venus'. However, he had not appeared on the bill since their failure in Cork, so the break-up may have occurred before she met Nelson. That said, while the two were in Newcastle in August, Mr. Warton certainly felt it necessary to place the following letter in the Newcastle Journal:

"THE WALHALLA ENTERTAINMENT. TO THE EDITOR OF THE NEWCASTLE JOURNAL, SIR, A Bill has been put into my Hands purporting to be a Programme of the Entertainment of Madam Warton, at your Theatre Royal. Perceiving that use is made of my name under the designation of Professor Warton, I beg respectfully to inform you, and also for the Information of the Public of Newcastle, to whom I feel deeply Indebted for their Patronage during my stay in your Town, that I am in no way connected with the Parties at present in Newcastle appearing under the Name of Madam Warton. The Insertion of this in your valuable Journal, will oblige, Sir, your obedient Servant, B. J. WARTON. 49, George Street, Euston Square, London, May 12th,

1853.[31]"

It seemed that there were now two troupes using the name of Madame Warton, one remaining in London, the other touring the country. Whatever the truth of the matter, any potential relationships between Nelson and Warton abruptly came to an end in January 1854. Hernandez and Stone, an American Circus that Nelson had close connections with, had engaged both for their tour. They were tenting on the Derby Arms Bowling Green, Chestergate in Macclesfield[32] where Madame Warton was playing her usual role as Lady Godiva and Nelson, Peeping Tom[33].

Unfortunately, Madame Warton caught a fever and died[34]. Later it was revealed that she had taken a room in a lodging house where the previous occupant had died of typhus fever[35]. She was buried in St. Paul's churchyard in Macclesfield[36]. The inscription on her headstone reads:

"SACRED
TO
THE MEMORY OF
ELIZA CROW
HER PROFESSIONAL NAME
MADAM WARTON
WHO DIED JAN 27TH 1854
AGED 27 YEARS.
THIS TABLET RAISED TO HER
MEMORY
BY A DEAR AND SINCERE
FRIEND
ARTHUR NELSON"

Given the circus connection it's very likely that Arthur Nelson had already taken over the effective management of the troupe, but following Eliza Crow's death this became clear. Above an announcement in the Era of the re-internment of Madame Warton, most likely placed by Nelson himself, we are told that the troupe, presently in Manchester, is "wholly under the Direction of Mr. Arthur Nelson[37]". However, his future plans did not lie with the troupe as he took a further advert, "TO MANAGERS of FIRST CLASS THEATRES ONLY" stating that he was, "now ready to engage as Clown in a Christmas Pantomime, as also a first-rate Pantaloon[38]". Irony has it that, in the same edition, Professor Warton also advertised the fact that his troupe, called "MDME WARTON'S WALHALLA" were also seeking a new engagement following their closure at the Royal Grecian, City-road[39].

Further advertisements in the Era of 26 August tell us more about both the troupe's situation, its size:

"THE MADAME WARTON'S unrivalled Troupe from the Walhalla, Leicester-square, performing now in Bury to crowded and delighted audiences. The Troupe consists of Fourteen Females, Six Males and Four Children, and patronised by the Earl of Stamford, Lord Milbank, Major

ELIZA CROW'S GRAVESTONE IN
MACCLESFIELD CEMETERY
(2010)

and Mayoress of Macclesfield, Mayor and ex-Mayor of Bolton within the last fortnight.

"PS. — The Troupe is under the management of Mr. ARTHUR NELSON, whose inimitable performance on the Rock Harmonicon, Pine Sticks, &c., never fail to draw thunders of applause. This company does not accept engagements, and is no way connected with any other Troupe ...[40]"

and Arthur's personal ambitions or desperation:

"NOTICE TO AUSTRALIAN MANAGERS, Mr. ARTHUR NELSON, Clown King, is open to make an Engagement as Stage Clown, and Produce Pantomimes, or Equestrian Clown, or Low Comedian Performer on the Monstre Dolcimello, Rock Harmonicon, Musical Pine Sticks, Steel Bars, China Plates, Musical Glasses and Clay Pantiles. As also Stage Manager in an Amphitheatre, having a thorough knowledge of Stage and Ring Business, from Richard III down to Billy Button.[41]"

Arthur was to neither go to Australia nor pick up a pantomime that season. He was still with the Warton troupe in Goole at the end of November and resorted to doing his favourite stunt on the river[42]. By February 1855 he was touring Ireland with Bell's American Circus.

It is clear that Madame Warton's troupe enjoyed significant, if brief, status within the popular culture of the period. Her shows in Leicester Square at the Walhalla were for family viewing, with specific morning opening times so that all could have the possibility of attending. The concept was to make high art available to a wider public. The performance itself was more than simply standing still. Professional actors had to develop and hold their bodies motionless for potentially long periods. The skill and training needed to do this might be compared with that of a ballet dancer. That said, motion was also involved, with Madame Warton, towards the end of the 1840s, advertising 'moving' tableaux vivants. Indeed, one writer had pointed out that, "Movement was a central part of the tableau vivant performance in a variety of ways. To begin with, arrangements were frequently chosen that exaggerated the perception of arrested movement and increased the danger of performers dropping the pose. ... In the professional theatre, motionless, posed performers were moved around by stage machinery in order to enhance the view of the audience. By the middle of the century, a circular revolving pedestal was being used to rotate statuary groups such as the Three Graces, enabling theatre audiences to simulate the spatial experience of walking round sculpture in a gallery, as well as offering the optimum visibility of the bodies on display.[43]"

The weakness of this performance art was that it could be easily mimicked and degraded by those who wanted to provide 'down-market' versions to appeal to the lower orders of society. One unabashed exponent of this was Renton Nicholson who styled himself 'Lord Chief Baron Nicholson' and ran the 'Judge and Jury Club', an entertainment that provided mock-trials of the rich and famous dependent on the scandals of the day. He ran the Coal Hole Tavern in the Strand next to the Surrey Theatre. His establishment offered "Poses Plastiques Every Evening, at Half Past Seven and After the Theatres supported by the most exquisite models.[44]". That said, advertising for the Warton's troupe often appealed to the baser instincts as pointed out by the Coventry Herald journalist, who in a very supportive piece ended with:

"If we might be allowed to offer one word of suggestion to Madame Warton, we should say, by all means leave out those pictorial representations from the posting-bills, which help to give force to objections made outside the Theatre, which would never be made within, by those who had witnessed the exhibition. Even the more finished pictures of Madame Warton herself do no justice to the original, and only tend to deceive and give a lower impression of the exhibition than

PEEPING TOM OF COVENTRY
Gentleman's Magazine July 1826, p.20.

would otherwise be received.[45]"

Despite this, the people of Coventry took Madame Warton to their hearts, and on her final performance in 1848 presented her with a gold watch:

"… a most elegant and superbly finished piece of workmanship. The dial is of bright and dead gold, chastely executed, and ornamented with our national emblems, the rose shamrock and thistle. On the back of the inner case is an admirable engraving of her own personation of Lady Godiva in the tableau. The inside of the outer case bears the inscription, 'Presented to Madame Warton by her friends in Coventry, as an admiring tribute to her classic genius and artistic merit.' On the back of the outer case is very beautifully engraved the city arms of Coventry, the elephant and castle.[46]"

Ultimately, maintaining representations of high-art in physical form was highly dependent on the audience recognising the original piece it was drawn from. Warton's modelling for Landseer[47] and her performance as Lady Godiva, a well-known story that appealed to Victorian sensibilities, enabled her to move beyond this simple premise and gain something of celebrity status. That said, by the time of her last performance in a circus, where she played Godiva and Nelson, Peeping Tom[48], her 'chef-d'oeuvre' had become more parody than pastiche.

---

[1] Edinburgh Evening Courant — 24 January 1828, p.3.

[2] Ibid. — 28 January 1828, p.3.

[3] North Wales Chronicle — 17 February 1835, p.4.

[4] Cummingham, A. (1843) The Life of Sir David Wilkie with His Journals, Tours and Critical Remarks on Works of Art and a Selection from his Correspondence Vol II. p.333.

[5] Ibid. p.409.

[6] Ibid. p.415.

[7] London Standard — 18 January 1833, p.1.

[8] Morning Post — 27 August 1830, p.3.

[9] Ibid. — 25 October 1830, p.3. – "Mr. FERDINARD FLOR much pleased the Royal Party and Visitors by a skilful representation of pictures of the best Masters, by living subjects."

[10] Ibid. — 18 June 1832, p.1. – "FINE ARTS.– Mr. FERDINAND FLOR begs leave to inform the Nobility, the Public, and his Friends, that her Most Gracious MAJESTY'S PORTRAIT, painted in full length, in her Coronation Robes, is now exposed to public VIEW at the Pautechnicon."

[11] Morning Chronicle — 26 November 1834, p.4. – James Thoms sculpted statues of Tam O'Shanter and Souter Johnnie in 1828. These were eventually placed within the Burn's monument at Alloway but had toured Britain beforehand reaching London in April 1829.

[12] Head, J.H. (1860) Home Pastimes, or Tableau Vivants. p.14.

[13] The Era — 24 September 1854, p.1. – "THEATRE ROYAL, HUDDERSFIELD. — Monday, 25, and during the week. Madame Warton's Troupe, from the Walhalla, Leicester-square, having terminated a most successful week in Halifax, commence their classical representations at the Theatre, Ramsden-street. Nelson the Clown King, and Comic Thunderer, will storm the audience with his witty Reminiscences. P.S. – Wanted, Two first rate Female Models and a Singing Chambermaid."

[14] Ibid. 8 — 8 October 1846, p.1.

[15] Ibid. 13 — 12 May 1847, p.1.

[16] Ibid. — 16 May 1847, p.11.

[17] Ibid. 8 — 11 October 1847, p.3.

[18] Ibid. 15 — 2 January 1848, p.12. – Landseer did not complete the picture until 1865.

[19] The role of Lady Godiva from 1677 was often played by a boy and only in 1842 was it suggested that the person playing the role be dressed in keeping with the story. A flesh coloured dress was the compromise and the name of the "Lady" who played Godiva was kept secret to protect her reputation.

[20] Coventry Standard — 2 June 1848, p.4. – "Mr. Batty, of the Circus Royal or Astley's Amphitheatre, had most liberally offered a beautiful Milk White Steed to carry the representative of GODIVA, the benefactress of Coventry; and an application has, we hear, been made to the Lady who has personated that character with so much applause and admiration in the celebrated Tableaux Vivians, in London, to undertake it here on this occasion."

[21] Newcastle Journal — 31 March 1849, p.2.

[22] Ibid. 13 — Sunday 29 April 1849, p.1. – "Madame Warton respectfully informs the Public and her Country Friends that she is not in any way connected with any other Establishment of a similar kind."

[23] Newcastle Guardian and Tyne Mercury — 15 September 1849, p.4.

[24] The troupe was to open at the Theatre Royal, Cork on 9 January 1851. But according to the Southern Reporter and Cork Commercial Courier — 11 January 1851 p.2. – " … when the appointed hours for the opening of the doors arrived, the few persons who presented themselves for admission were informed, we have heard, that Madam's travelling carriage met with an accident which delayed her arrival, and that therefore there would be no 'exhibition' on that evening. Report, however attributed the disappointment to the interference of his Worship the Mayor, who it is alleged, prohibited the Theatre being opened, because as was stated, the usual etiquette of asking his permission had been neglected by the Manager. This statement we are authorised to say is correct, as his Worship did not at all interfere beyond giving the usual permission sought for in such cases."

[25] Southern Reporter and Cork Commercial Courier — 25 February 1851, p.3.

[26] Reynolds's Newspaper — 30 March 1851, p.9.

[27] Ibid. 15 — 8 August 1852, p.1. – "STANDARD THEATRE, SHOREDITCH, On Monday, and all week, to begin with THE SEVENTH VICTIM; or The Murder at the Dog and Duck … After which, a classical entertainment in which the original and celebrated MADAME WARTON and TROUPE, from the Walhalla, will appear in their Classical Groupings, represented on white marble, and illuminated by the electric light, under the direction of Mr. Morgan. To conclude with TURPIN'S RIDE TO YORK, in which a splendid stud of horses, and Mr. Harwood, and his celebrated mare, Black Bess, will appear."

[28] Lloyd's Weekly Newspaper — August 1852, p.10.

[29] Ibid. 13 — 29 August 1852, p.1.

[30] Ibid. — 2 January 1853, p.12.

[31] Newcastle Journal — 21 May 1853, p.1.

[32] Manchester Times — 14 January 1854, p.7.

[33] Ibid. — 21 January 1854, p.12. – "On Wednesday evening, the performances were under the patronage of the mayor, John Smith, Esq.; and the tent was crowded to excess. Also on Thursday night, for the benefit of Nelson, the 'Clown King,' the house was again crowded. Madame Wharton appeared as 'Lady Godiva,' and Nelson as 'Peeping Tom'."

[34] Manchester Courier and Lancashire General Advertiser — 11 February 1854, p.7.

[35] Leamington Spa Courier — 4 February 1854, p.3. – "DEATH OF MADAME WARTON. — this well known lady has met with an untimely fate at Macclesfield, in consequence of sleeping in lodgings that had been infected with typhus fever. She took the disease immediately, and died on Friday morning after a week's illness."

[36] Ibid. 13 — 6 August 1854, p.1. – "THE LATE and MUCH LAMENTED MADAME WARTON has been re-interred in St. Paul's Churchyard, Macclesfield, Cheshire. A splendid Monument, with the Statue of Eve at the Fountain, adorns the Grave, while a Drooping Elm o'erhangs the Resting-place of this once-admired Artist. The expenses were defrayed from the Private Purse of Mr. Arthur Nelson."

[37] Ibid.

[38] Ibid.

[39] Ibid.

[40] Ibid. 13 — 27 August 1854, p.1.

[41] Ibid.

[42] Hull Packet - Friday 08 December 1854, p.6. – "NOVEL RIDE. — On Thursday, the 30th ult., Mr. Arthur Nelson, the clown with Madame Wharton's troupe of poses plastiques, had a ride on the river in a washing tub, drawn by four geese."

[43] Nead, L. (2008) The Haunted Gallery: Painting, Photography and Film c. 1900, p.71-72.

[44] Bell's Life in London and Sporting Chronicle — 9 November 1856, p.2.

[45] Coventry Herald — 20 October 1848, p.4.

[46] Ibid. 19 — 1 December 1848, p.4.

[47] Since the painting was not finished until 1865, no-one would have seen the result in her lifetime.

[48] An addition to the legend says that a tailor took a peep at Lady Godiva during her ride and was struck blind. "This circumstance is commemorated to the present day, by a grotesque figure called Peeping Tom, which appears looking out of a corner window of opening in a wall, in Smithfold-street. It is about six-feet in height, and is an ancient full-length statue of a man in plate-armour, with skirts. It is carved with a pedestal, from a single block of oak, and the back is hollowed out, in order to render it less ponderous. The crest of the helmet is nearly destroyed, and the arms were cut-off at the elbows, in order to favour its present position of leaning out of the window." — The Gentleman's Magazine — July 1826, p.21-22.

8

The Aztec Lilliputians

In 1859 Arthur Nelson was to be engaged to provide musical accompaniment to a show and exhibition in South Wales and Ireland[1]. This 'act', known in Britain as the 'Aztec Lilliputians', had arrived from America in 1853. It comprised of two diminutive children suffering from, what was later known as, microcephaly, which resulted in misshapen heads. They were displayed following a 'lecture' on their supposed origins. During the 1850s, this exhibition, despite some controversy, was extremely popular. The 'Aztecs' were seen by hundreds of thousands of people, gained audiences with the American President, Queen Victoria and a host of other European royalty.

It has been suggested that the 'Aztec Lilliputians' was one of Barnum's elaborate hoaxes[2], although in reality his involvement with the act was much later in their career. The proprietors of these two individuals suggested they were from a lost tribe of Aztecs that had been discovered and brought back from Central America. This story was backed up by apocryphal 'evidence' from a pamphlet[3] sold at the performances. The account, written in the third person, draws on 'the journal of Pedro Velasquez', an indigo trader from Central America. The forty-page volume also references the work of John Stephens, a respected American explorer and archaeologist, who was the first to draw the public's attention to the Mayan civilisation in Central America. In a number of works he referred to an ancient un-discovered city:

"Beyond was a wilderness, stretching off to the Lake of Peten, and that region of Lacandones, or unbaptized Indians, in which, according to the suggestion made in my previous volumes, lay that mysterious city never reached by a white man, but still occupied by Indians precisely in the same state as before the discovery of America.[4]"

In an earlier book, John Stephens had told a story related to him by an old padre of this 'living city' where the occupants still spoke Maya and continued to practise the customs of the civilisation destroyed by the Spanish invasion:

"He had heard it many years before at the village of Chajul, and was told by the villagers that from the topmost ridge of the sierra this city was distinctly visible. He was then young, and with much labour climbed to the naked summit of the sierra, from which, at a height of ten or twelve thousand feet, he looked over an immense plain extending to Yucatan and the Gulf of Mexico, and saw at a great distance a large city spread over a great space, and with turrets white and glittering in the sun.[5]"

Clearly, Stephens wanted to believe in this story:

"… and, as he drew a map on the table, and pointed out the sierra to the top of which he had climbed, and the position of the mysterious city, the interest awakened in us was the most thrilling I ever experienced. One look at that city was worth ten years of an everyday life. If he is right, a place is left where Indians and an Indian city existed as Cortez and Alvarado found them; there are living men who can solve the mystery that hangs over the ruined cities of America; perhaps who can go to Copan and read the inscriptions on the monuments. No subject more exciting and attractive presents itself to my mind, and the deep impression of that night will never be effaced.[6]"

This provided the back-story for Velasquez's tale.

The 'memoir' goes on to state that two North Americans, named Huertis and Hammond, intrigued by Stephen's passages, decided to try and find this undiscovered city. On their way, they meet Pedro Velasquez and introduce him to the first of Stephens's books and when shown the engravings it contained:

"He recognized many of them as old acquaintances, others as new ones, which had escaped his more cursory inspection; in all he could trace curious details which, on the spot, he regretted the want of time to examine. … When Mr. Huertis read to him the further account of the information given to Mr. Stephens by the jolly and merry, but intelligent old padre of Quiche, respecting other ruined cities beyond the Sierra Madre, and especially of the living city of the Candones, or unchristianized Indians, supposed to have been seen from the lofty summit of that mountain range, and was told by Messrs Huertis and Hammond that the exploration of this city was the chief object of their perilous expedition, the senor adds, that his enthusiasm became enkindled

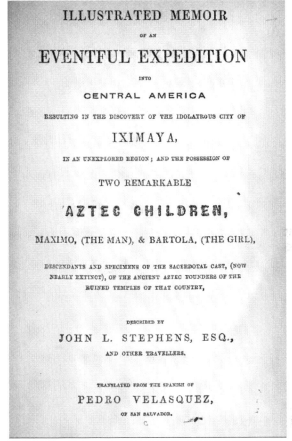

ILLUSTRATED MEMOIR

OF AN

EVENTFUL EXPEDITION

INTO

CENTRAL AMERICA

RESULTING IN THE DISCOVERY OF THE IDOLATROUS CITY OF

IXIMAYA,

IN AN UNEXPLORED REGION; AND THE POSSESSION OF

TWO REMARKABLE

'AZTEC CHILDREN,

MAXIMO, (THE MAN), & BARTOLA, (THE GIRL),

DESCENDANTS AND SPECIMENS OF THE SACERDOTAL CAST, (NOW
NEARLY EXTINCT), OF THE ANCIENT AZTEC FOUNDERS OF THE
RUINED TEMPLES OF THAT COUNTRY,

DESCRIBED BY

JOHN L. STEPHENS, ESQ.,

AND OTHER TRAVELLERS.

TRANSLATED FROM THE SPANISH OF

PEDRO VELASQUEZ,

OF SAN SALVADOR.

INNER TITLE OF ILLUSTRATED MEMOIR
OF AN EVENTFUL EXPEDITION INTO
CENTRAL AMERICA

to at least as high a fervour as theirs …"

After much tribulation, Huertis, Hammond and Velasquez enter the city of Iximaya and were given quarters in:

"the vacant wing of a spacious and sumptuous structure, at the western extremity of the city, which had been appropriated, from time immemorial, to the surviving remnant of an ancient and singular order of priesthood called Kaanas, which, it was distinctly asserted in their annals and traditions, had accompanied the first migration of this people from the Assyrian plains. Their peculiar and strongly distinctive lineaments, it is now perfectly well ascertained, are to be traced in many of the sculptured monuments of the central American ruins, and were found still more abundantly on those of Iximaya. Forbidden, by inviolably sacred laws, from intermarrying with any persons but those of their own caste, they had here dwindled down, in the course of many centuries, to a few insignificant individuals, diminutive in stature. They were, nevertheless, held in high veneration and affection by the whole Iximayan community, probably as living specimens of an antique race nearly extinct.[8]"

Velasquez relates how he made friends with the guardian of one of these individuals, who helped him escape, while Hammond died of wounds inflicted on entry to the city and Huertis became a human sacrifice "upon the high altar of the sun". On his return to San Salvador, the two 'Aztec children', who were given the names Maximo and Bartola, "became objects of the highest interest to the most intellectual classes of that city. As the greatest ethnological curiosities in living form that ever appeared among civilised men, he was advised to send them to Europe for exhibition.[9]"

The book ends with the following claim and invitation:

"In brief, these Aztec Children present the most extraordinary phenomenon in the human race ever witnessed by the modern world: let their origin be what it may — let their history and their country's history be ever so vague and traditionary — doubt the truth of Velasquez's narrative or believe it wholly — these children present in themselves the eighth wonder of the world. They are, without exception, the most remarkable and intensely interesting objects that were ever presented to the European public.

"In America they have been the marvel of a million beholders, and wherever they travel they must become the centre of attraction of every inquiring mind, and will doubtless prove a puzzle to the profoundest philosophers and ethnologists of the age.

"All the learned and scientific men in the United States have submitted them to critical examination, and unite in pronouncing them the most unique and extraordinary beings that have ever fallen under observation.

"The attention of European men of science, ethnologists, physiologists, philosophers, and physicians, is now called to these most curious and remarkable children. They are requested to examine and fully investigate what the scientific men of America have united in pronouncing the most startling and extraordinary curiosity that has been exhibited in the present century.[10]"

The claims, as one might expect, were not entirely true. The New York Herald, attacking the exhibition of the children as "The Aztec Humbug", stated:

"The true history of these dwarfs, who are simply a pair of accidental idiots from Central America, is well known to many persons in this city. The 'Aztec Children,' as they are called by their showman, were found running about the streets of Granada or Leon, or some other small town in Central America, about the month of May, 1850, by a man named John Addison, formerly a jeweller of San Francisco, Cal, who conceived the idea that money might be made by their exhibition, and who, in connection with a native of Central America, named Selva, purchased them from an old woman for an ounce of gold, with a promise to give her a portion the profits. They brought them to this city, where they arrived in the month of July, 1850. Mr Addison took rooms at the Howard Hotel, then called 'Barnum's' where these deformed, disgusting objects were seen by a large number of persons. There was no pretence made at that time that these 'Aztecs' as they have since been nicknamed were other that a couple of deformed, idiotic children, the offspring of a negro father and a miserably and besotted Indian mother; and in proof, of this they were exhibited at the Minerva Rooms, in Broadway, by Mr. Addison, during the months of September or October, 1850, and were called, as the bills will show, 'Indian Dwarfs from Central America.' Not more than a dozen persons attended the exhibition, and Addison, finding it would not pay, sold or leased the monstrosities to William Raymond, as we are informed — the great showman of wild beasts. They were afterwards exhibited in Boston, Albany, and Troy, without success; and it is since that period, and their return here, that, under the present manager, the absurd story of their origin and connection with the old Aztec race of kings or priests has been manufactured, by a well known person in this city, formally employed by Moses Y. Beach, and published in the Journal of Commerce, to humbug and astound the good people of this city out of their shillings, by the impudent fabrication of their capture, flight, and wonderful history.

"This is a true and veritable statement of this gross humbug, and the reason of the base attempt to assail us because we refused to become an associate of their infamy — all which we are ready to prove by a cloud of witnesses.[11]"

Indeed in July 1852, the Herald's journalism was corroborated by a legal investigation in Philadelphia:

"Some light has been thrown upon the history of the 'Aztec Children' lately on exhibition in this city, by a legal investigation held in Philadelphia, a Mr. Silva claiming them on behalf of their parents in Central America. From his testimony it appears that the parents are living in the village of Jacota in the state of San Salvador. In 1849 he obtained possession of the children under the promise of educating them at Grenada, but gave them up at San Carlo Nicaragua to his brother-in-law, Salaza, who brought them to the United States in company with Mr. Addison, an American. The parents have since, hearing that the children had been sold, demanded them of Silva, who was put by the magistrates of Grenada under bonds to bring them back again. Hence his application to the Court at Philadelphia: — 'The Judge held that he could not interfere with the present custody of the children, upon the unsupported testimony of the witness alone. He had evidently parted with their custody to his brother-in-law (Mr. Salaza) and until it could be shown that the children were not cared for according to the original agreement between witness and the parents of the children, the court would not interfere.' They therefore remain in the custody of their exhibitor, Mr. Morris. We do not know whether these sturdy revelations are likely to disturb the belief of our city newspapers in their editorial opinions set forth a few months since of a new race of beings, the mysterious 'Aztec' origin and other absurdities broached in advertisements and an amusing pamphlet sold at the exhibition room of those 'monstrosities.'[12]"

The Herald had a good track record for exposing hoaxes right back to 1835. The competitive cauldron of the New York press tempted journalists to invent stories in order to sell newspapers. In 1835, the 'Great Moon Hoax' was perpetuated by The Sun newspaper, when in a series of tantalising statements and articles it claimed that Sir John Herschel, the famous Scottish astronomer, had built a huge new telescope at the Cape of Good Hope. This was followed up by a series of extracts purportedly reprinted from a supplement to the Edinburgh Journal of Science. These 'quotations', albeit, long and rambling, gave a telescopic tour across the surface of the moon. The descriptions drew the readers in with each episode, firstly convincing them of the extreme power of the new technology, and eventually revealing plant and then increasingly sophisticated animal life, from 'biped beavers' who walked upright, carried their young in their arms and lived in huts, to the 'Vespertilio-homo', or 'man-bat'. In the fifth article Herschel 'discovered' 'an abandoned temple' made of sapphire with a roof of yellow metal made to look like a mass of flames rising upwards and licking at a large sphere of clouded copper. The author of the moon hoax was Richard Adams Locke, the then editor of the Sun, and despite having given up journalism in 1842 was the person referred to as the "well known person in this city, formally employed by Moses Y. Beach[13]". Locke had tried to perpetuate another hoax in 1837, while editor of the New Era, by publishing the lost diary of Mungo Park. Park was a famed Scottish explorer who had disappeared on an expedition into the heart of Africa in 1806. The 'Lost Manuscript of Mungo Park' had been 'found' by another British explorer in Africa thirty years later. The hoax was a monumental flop as New Yorkers were by then wise to Locke's reputation. The New Era was soon closed having failed to increase its circulation.

At the time, Locke denied being the author of the *Illustrated Memoir of the Eventful Expedition into Central America*[14] and his authorship has never been conclusively proved. However, there are clear similarities in the nature and form of the story with his earlier hoaxes – the existence of an impossible to verify 'journal', and the 'borrowing' of the credibility of the leading expert to perpetuate the hoax are but two.

What made Maximo and Bartola unique from other exhibitions and therefore enabled their story to be accepted by the public in America and Britain was that they remained an enigma, both to the scientific community and those that paid to see them. For those that visited the shows it was their charm and innocence that was often beguiling:

"We have taken our wife and children to see them, and will to do so again, and we mean to persuade our friends to go and see them. And we shall do

OUTLINE ILLUSTRATIONS

FROM THE

RUINS OF CENTRAL AMERICA

OF ITS

ANCIENT RACES.

The accompanying engravings, sketched from the ruins of Central America, bear both in features and in position of the head, a resemblance all will readily detect to the Aztec children, found in the same country, and now being exhibited ; and who according to succeeding pages, belong to an ancient sacerdotal caste.

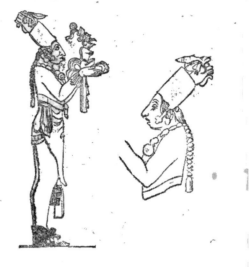

OUTLINE ILLUSTRATIONS FROM THE
RUINS OF CENTRAL AMERICA OF ITS
ANCIENT RACES
Illustrated Memoir Of An Eventful Expedition
Into Central America

this, not because we believe them the descendants of any race or tribe, or class, or caste, that have never been seen or heard of by civilized man but simply because they are the most beautiful, gentle, playful, and happy little curious creatures that have ever bore the human form.[15]"

J. M. Morris, the exhibitor and guardian of the children, relied on the curiosity, belief in the probable, and scepticism of the public, in order to attract an audience. He had perfected his technique by the time they came to Britain, as demonstrated by the advertisements he placed in local newspapers:

"There is no time to be lost. All those who feel curious concerning these Wonders of Creation — all who are desirous, or who are willing to be convinced that there is in existence a distant race of human beings, new to the present age, as beautiful as they are diminutive, as extraordinary as they are incomprehensible, will hasten to the Music-Hall, and see what the Aztec Lilliputians are — in their presence, scepticism will be dissipated. It is impossible to believe that they are that which they really are unless they are seen. The fact is admitted that it is out of the power of pen or tongue to describe

THESE ASTONISHING AND GRACEFUL BEINGS,

who have no resemblance but to the Sculptured Marbles of Nineveh, Egypt and Central America.[16]"

Charles Dickens was not fooled by the story of Iximaya, nor the origins of the children. He visited the exhibition in July 1853 and, as well as demolishing the 'memoir'[17], described the form the presentation took:

"More we need scarcely say about the fable coined to heighten the attraction of the dwarf children. They are, doubtless, a couple of dwarf children, bought from Indians, and made into a show. When we went to see them, a candid gentleman told to the assembled visitors the Velasquez story, in an artless and ingenuous way, that oiled its passage into our heads. He acknowledged that it looked here and there rather incredible, but there it was, just as it came to him: Velasquez might be a great cheat, but he hoped not; if he was, it was a pity. All they knew was — there were the children.

"A gentleman who seemed to be the guardian-in-chief then stepped forward, and with still greater candour and liberality began thus: — 'Gentlemen and ladies, with the story just told to you, we have nothing at all to do'[18]"

Dickens with incredulity gave his thoughts at this moment:

"— at that we halted somewhat. Why then did you write Aztec Lilliputians on our tickets? Why did you placard London with coloured tableaux representing atomies on pillars being worshipped, desperate and picturesque assaults, and so on, all belonging to the story that has just been told us? Why did not the flaming picture of the show outside correspond to the reality within? The gentleman disclaimed, however, all responsibility for the story. If it were false, what is the truth? As for him, there were the children. Account for them in any way, and still were they not wonders? If their guardians had meant to palm a tale upon the public they could easily have manufactured a Velasquez, and produced him. So on.[19]"

At this point the children themselves were introduced to the audience and Dickens describes how the audience reacted:

"They began their performance by running very obediently together, like horses in a circus, round the long platform in the middle of the room. Then they were put upon the platform and played monkey tricks for the amusement of the public, which assembled round them very much as it collects about the monkeys at Regent's Park, and gave them cakes, and differed chiefly in its behaviour from the same public looking at monkeys, in the common manifestation of a desire to kiss them.

"Next to kissing, the chief pleasure seemed to consist in feeling their heads. They are not themselves by any means so small as they are represented to be on the bills out of doors. In those bills they are shown as veritable Lilliputians, perched like sparrows upon columns, or 'as exhibited before Her Majesty;' of dimensions that would allow them to stand comfortably in the hat held by one of the suite who is looking on. Bodily they are three feet high; but their heads are disproportionately small, instead of being disproportionately large, as dwarfs' heads usually are. They are like dolls' heads, and so of course it is agreeable to feel them.[20]"

Dickens then reveals the 'plants' in the audience, as the showmen worked the audience:

"Her Majesty's name was judiciously introduced into the entertainment; and it was dexterously suggested to us that many ladies come repeatedly to observe whether the children make any progress as the days roll on. Perhaps that was the case of an enthusiastic lady, who made the air alive with cries of 'Kiss me, darling—Come, Maximo, dear— kiss me, dear—O (to her friend, another lady), he is very much improved.' Some cheap toys had been put forward from a hand or two about the room—one of them a cat capable of squeaking. Maximo was causing it to squeak. 'What's that,' asked the lady. 'Isn't it a cat? Say cat. Say cat, de—ar !' Maximo at last was persuaded to obey. 'It's the first time,' said the lecturer, in an interested way, 'that I have heard him pronounce the word—cat.' We were all, of course, thrilled with interest.

"Then there was a little boy who played with the children, and carried round the Illustrated History of the Aztec Lilliputians, price one shilling, with all the startling tableaux in it; and who seemed too much at home to be a page. He began walking round the platform with a 'Daguerreotype picture of the Aztec Lilliputians, only half a guinea,' and our ears deceived us if it was not the rapturous lady who told him that he was a silly fellow, and that it couldn't be sold to-night; certainly it was the rapturous lady's

DAGUERREOTYPE OF THE AZTEC CHILDREN, TAKEN BY
BECKERS & PIARD OF NEW YORK, CA. 1850
Pratt Museum Papers, Amherst College Archives & Special
Collections

friend who scolded him sotto voce — we happened to stand close by — and told him that if his father heard him he would be very angry. Nevertheless he went off to try a little unobtrusive bargaining in another corner.

"... Maximo was being asked to sit down. Presently he squatted with his legs turned out in idol attitude. 'O,' cried the enthusiastic lady, 'that's the way he was worshipped! I am sure of it. I am sure,' turning to her friend, but speaking so that every one might hear her, though in a low voice, 'I am sure he was worshipped as a god, sitting in that way.' After a little more such entertainment we departed.[21]"

Dickens' contempt at the gullibility of those that attended is palpable, and only surpassed by the audacity of those that exploited it:

"If these children had been exhibited as American dwarfs, (as, for example, the abnormal offspring of a Hebrew father and a mulatto mother; which they are as likely as not to be), however much we might have deplored the taste of the town in gathering about them with sponge cake and kisses, we should have quietly submitted to the passing folly. We are disposed to think, however, that a grave social topic is involved, whenever we observe success in any gross attempt to practise upon public credulity. As for gullibility itself, that, we suppose, will last among us till the schoolmaster shall have his own. It is a vulnerable part that we cannot remove; nevertheless we may defend it from barefaced attack.[22]"

Morris never claimed their existence proved the story told in the 'memoir', indeed his greater concern was to counter any accusation that the two individuals were 'dwarfs'. What made them different from other exhibitions was the supposition they were a unique 'race' or 'species' of man. Scientific recognition, in a period when different theories about man, creation and species abounded, made the individuals far more valuable as exhibits. The invitation to men of science was a direct consequence of this and, if the scientific community could be persuaded to engage in debate concerning the children, it could be exploited. The arrival of the 'Aztecs' led to a special meeting of the Ethnological Society on 6 July to examine the children. Key to this meeting was the opinion of Sir Richard Owen, the foremost expert on anatomy and Professor of Anatomy and Conservator at the Royal College of Surgeons. The London Standard reported that this meeting had "disabused the pubic mind" of the fanciful story of their origin and "that the opinion which has been circulated that they represent a distinct branch of the human family is wholly without warrant. ... Professor Owen is 'inclined to look at them as instances of impeded development'.[23]"

Despite this, advertisements continued to describe the children as an ancient race, and in future editions of the 'memoir' a 'testimonial' from Richard Owen was printed as if he gave his approval:

"PROFESSOR OWEN, the first comparative anatomist of the age, in one of his letters addressed to the guardians of these little strangers, after returning thanks for the opportunity and facilities afforded him in his examination of them, says: –

"'The remarkable difference which these extraordinary children present, as compared with normal European children, with analogous stages of dentition[24], in thin and slender stature, and especially in the smaller proportion of the cranial part of the head, renders them objects of peculiar interest to the physiologist and naturalist; whilst their quick perceptive faculties, their full dark eyes, their deep olive complexion, and the singularity of some of their attitudes, combine to invest them with a character of peculiar singularity, which cannot fail to gratify and surprise beholders.'

"'Professor Owen concurs with the learned physicians of Charleston, South Carolina whose testimonial was submitted to him by Mr. Morris, in the opinion that these children manifest no characters which ally them more closely than other human beings to the brute creation. The learned physicians state that they do not believe these people are dwarfs.

"'Museum, Royal College of Surgeons, London, June 30th, 1853

"'J.M. Morris, Esq.'[25]"

As Dickens had stated, the presentation of the children to Queen Victoria on 4 July was also ruthlessly exploited. Further editions of the 'memoir' having a dedication to Prince Albert, which carefully suggested his interest was purely scientific.

"TO
HIS ROYAL HIGHNESS
PRINCE ALBERT,
AS THE PATRON OF SCIENCE
AND THE
PROMOTER OF WHATEVER TENDS TO THE KNOWLEDGE
AND
INTERESTS OF HUMANITY
THIS
LITTLE SKETCH OF THE AZTECS' HISTORY
IS, WITH SENTIMENTS OF
PROFOUND RESPECT AND EXTREME GRATITUDE,
MOST HUMBLY DEDICATED."

THE AZTEC LILLIPUTIANS WITH THEIR
MANAGER.
Wellcome Library, London ICV No 7592.

By early 1854, the truth regarding the origin of the children was being widely reported in local newspapers in towns and cities where they were appearing. As doubts arose, Morris felt obliged to issue a statement, in which he accused his rivals of wanting the children for themselves and giving a different explanation as to why the New York Herald had called the show a 'humbug':

"A CARD. — FROM THE GUARDIAN OF THE AZTEC LILLIPUTIANS. – Mr. J.M. MORRIS, Guardian of the Aztecs, in order to disabuse the public mind in regard to these little folk, begs to state that the various stories now circulating in Manchester in regard to their birth, parentage, abiding place &c. are but revived ones published in America through the instigation of the Spaniards from whom he procured them, and proved before the Court of Oyer and Terminer, in Philadelphia city, Judge Thompson presiding, in the year 1851, to be entirely erroneous; ... The only inquiry is as to the cause of these continued publications; and the answer is, that certain Spaniards want either to get hold of the Aztecs, or to prevent their successful exhibition by others. The public are assured that the guardian of the Aztecs has no desire or reason to thrust Velasquez's story of the Aztecs upon them. This much the press everywhere admits. ... Now as regards their being interesting and agreeable, just before they left America, and after all that could be done both by the Spaniards and James Gordon Bennett, of the New York Herald, the former being desirous of repossessing the children (which the court of Philadelphia refused), and the latter as affidavits show, on account of Mr. Morris not giving his bill and job printing to the *Herald* office ...[26]"

Despite this, the lecture and exhibition continued to attract large audiences including presentations at schools throughout Manchester[27].

The display of Maximo and Bartola was to continue for the next half century. The pair toured Europe where they appeared before Emperor Napoleon III in Paris, then on to Russia, Prussia, Bavaria, the Netherlands, Belgium, Flanders and Brabant and on their eventual return to America they were engaged by Barnum at his American Museum. One might wonder why the story surrounding the 'Aztecs' retained its interest in the public eye. Morris summed up its attraction when asked whether he believed it himself, saying:

"I think the story is no more marvellous than the children themselves, as every body admits who sees them; and whether true or false, it is much sought after, because of its very strangeness; and as long as the world can be entertained by the Arabian Nights, Gulliver's Travels, or the like, the history of the Aztecs cannot fail to be generally read.[28]"

Interest in the two waned as they got older and by the time Arthur Nelson was part of their entertainment in 1859 they required additional support. This was provided by the 'Earthmen', Martinis and Flora; two diminutive

BOY AND GIRL of THE EARTHMEN TRIBE, FROM
PORT NATAL
Illustrated London News 6 November 1852, p.372.

individuals "who have been rescued from the lowest depths of barbarism, and surrounded by the novel sights, sounds, and comforts of English civilisation[29]".

Martinis and Flora were also exhibited as a result of their size with the public being told that they were from a tribe of 'Earthmen' indigenous to South Africa. Here they "burrow in the ground, and hence derive their name. By burrowing, the reader must not understand that they dig and hide under the surface like rabbits, but they scratch hollows in the ground to shield them in a measure from the wind. These hollows they line with a little straw, and then cover themselves with a slight grass mat, out of which they project their feet towards a fire, which burns in the centre of the hollows. A mat is hung to windward by the aid of two rods spread perpendicularly, and another mat fastened to a third rod, is spread horizontally over the hollow. This is all the protection the Earthmen possess against the heavy dews and atmospheric changes of night. In the morning they roll up their mats, and as they have neither cattle nor cultivated grounds; and as they make no culinary utensils, the traveller may pass within a quarter of a mile of their rude and wretched encampment without discovering them. The Earthmen shun the face of the white man, and as they usually cower down behind some inequality in the ground, when they see one approach, they are seldom or never seen by Europeans.[30]"

They first appeared as exhibits in May 1853. In advertisements, the public are told, "it had been determined to exhibit them, with a view to raising a fund for their education and future maintenance. Being the only specimens seen here of a race rapidly becoming extinct, and possessing, from their peculiarities of habit, feature and dwarfish growth, a strong claim to the attention of those interested in the variations of the human race[31]". In preparation for this Mr. George, their 'guardian', had "taught them a few accomplishments, such as thrumming a tune or two on the pianoforte, and singing divers nigger melodies[32]".

The 'Aztecs' and 'Earthmen' had in fact been exhibited together as early as 1853 at the Cremorne Gardens[33] and from 1854 on their first tour of the United Kingdom. The billing of the Earthmen as "the last link in the human chain[34]" dropped any pretence about raising money for their future. The joint presentation simply cashed in on the 'legitimisation' of such shows to the middle classes in the name of 'science' in the myriad of ethnological theories before the publication of Darwin's Origins of the Species. Not all of the scientific community were prepared to stay quiet with regard to the exploitation of their research, the public, and the ethical and moral disregard for these children. Dr John Conolly, President of the Ethnological Society voiced his concerns at the British Association for the Advancement of Science meeting in September 1854:

"Dr. CONOLLY offered some observation, in which he suggested that such people as the Bosjesnians and others of a similar race could not be considered as in the lowest scale of human beings. A year or two ago two miserable little idiots were exhibited in this country, said to be specimens never seen or heard of before. They had no proper use of their limbs; they could not speak a single word, and had no capacity for the use of language. The result of their exhibition was the realisation of a large sum of money, though he hoped what had been done by that society would be such to make a similar fraudulent exhibition impossible at any future time. There was another exhibition of two children from the extreme south of Africa, called the Earthmen, who had an aptitude for learning, and could have acquired almost anything. When he saw people brought here from the extreme south as well as the north, and treated almost like animals, and when he considered had an organisation which might be improved, it became a question whether this nation did all it could for them; and whether they could not do more for those who, he could not doubt, in future ages, might form an important part of the history of our globe.[35]"

In another address to the Ethnological Society that year, entitled, The Ethnological Exhibitions of London, he further commented:

"One would hope that they all occasionally breathe fresh air, and enjoy liberty in grassy fields; for six or seven hours' exhibition, six days in the week, in ill-ventilated rooms, however large, cannot be very favourable to their health.

"When looking, indeed, on these, or any other illustrations of Ethnology imported from other lands, it is impossible not to ask one's self what becomes of the illustrations when either the novelty of their exhibition has passed away, and the Town demands fresh wonders, or even when they have grown too big and troublesome to be carried about. The lives of the Aztecs have been insured by their proprietor, to whom they were sold like sheep; but what support is assured to them? Already they are falling into the class of minor shows, and exhibited in the suburbs. If they die, the exhibitor will receive the sum insured on their lives; if they outlive their popularity, what provision is made for them? In what workhouse will they end their days? The long-continued profits accruing from their exhibition, the rich presents, the boasted jewels showered upon them, — is anything secured from these to keep them in age, or when abandoned as no longer lucrative? ... During their long sojourn in this country, it is pitiable to see human beings stared at as mere objects of temporary amusement, to whose subsequent condition all are indifferent.[36]"

Conolly's fears were very much justified. During the tour of South Wales in 1859, of which Nelson was a part, Martinis, the 'Earthman', was to die of pneumonia at the King's Head Hotel in Neath on 29 April. He was buried in an unmarked grave in Llantwit cemetery the following Monday and the tour continued. Flora, now described as 'Miss FLORA, the Female of the Earthmen Tribe', continued to perform with Walter Morris, who managed the tour of South Wales and Ireland into the mid-1860s. Her last recorded performance with the 'Aztec Lilliputians' was in Liverpool in March 1864, "before their departure for America in April.[37]"

In 1867, when the 'Aztecs' returned to Britain an attempt to revive interest in their exhibition was made when they were married on 7 January 1867[38]. During the 1870s they gave 'receptions at home', or during intervals at other places of entertainment. At the Hippodrome in Paris, they were driven in a carriage made for Charles X of France and specially purchased for their entrance into the ring. During interludes in the general performance they gave receptions in the equestrian 'green room' for occupants of the boxes[39]. In the 1880s they were listed in Barnum and Bailey's Circus route books with their sixth 'owner', Mrs. Nellie March[40]. There is no record of their deaths.

The term 'Aztecs' or 'Estics' endured well into the twentieth century to describe microcephalic individuals appearing in circuses and sideshows throughout America and Europe. Perhaps the final use of the term was in reference to "Maggie, the Last of the Aztecs" who appeared in Tod Browning's 1932 film Freaks. 'Maggie' was actually a man and appeared in a number of films during the 1930s and 40s. His last performance was in 1968 at Dobritch International Circus at the Los Angeles Sports Arena[41].

Interest in the mysterious story of Iximaya and the 'Aztec' children's origin endured and was often repeated in magazines and family readers throughout the Victorian period[42] and even into the twentieth century[43].

---

[1] Nelson appeared with the Aztec Lilliputians and Earthmen from February to August 1859, first in South Wales and then in Ireland. In one advertisement we are told, "The music with the Aztec Exhibition will consist of Mr. Nelson, on the Rock and Stick Harmonicon. The Five Highland Bell Ringers in full costume. Pianoforte—Miss B. Butler; and Mr. Walter J. Morris, on the Crystal Ophonic." – Tipperary Vindicator — 24 June 1859, p.2.

[2] Evans R. T. (2010) Romancing the Maya: Mexican Antiquity in the American Imagination, 1820-1915, p.87 — "Barnum has found this pair of 'Aztecs' in El Salvador in 1849, and given their small stature (both stood just over three feet tall), it is believed they were either dwarves or victims of microcephaly, a disease that would have accounted for their somewhat, 'Aztec'-shaped heads."

[3] Anon. (1853) Illustrated Memoir of the Eventful Expedition into Central America Resulting in the Discovery of the Idolatrous City of Iximaya, in an Unexplored Region. – Between 1850 and 1867, fourteen editions at least of this volume were published in North America and Europe including German and French translations. There are few variations between them. This edition retrieved from http://www.archive.org/details/illustratedmemoiOOvela (last accessed 2 July 2015).

[4] Stephens, J. L. (1848) Incidents of travel in Yucatan Vol II. p.191.

[5] Stephens, J. L. (1845) Incidents of travel in Central America Vol II. p.195.

[6] Ibid. p.196.

[7] Ibid. 3 p.5.

[8] Ibid. p.24-25.

[9] Ibid. p.28.

[10] Ibid. p.36.

[11] New York Herald, 21 February 1852, p.3.

[12] The Literary World: A Journal of American and Foreign Literature, Science and Arts — 17 July 1852 No. 285, p.40.

[13] Moses Yale Beach had bought the Sun from his brother-in-law, Benjamin Day, in 1838.

[14] Ibid. 12 — 11 August 1853 – "Our readers may remember the absurd story which heralded their exhibition in this city, and which was attributed to no less an artist than the celebrated author of the 'Moon hoax,' though it is but justice to that gentleman to mention, that a manuscript letter from him, denying the authorship of the ridiculous invention, was circulated at the time."

[15] New York Daily Tribune — 23 February 1853, p.4. — this is a quote from "a paper in this City" in reply to a statement in The Philadelphia Bulletin which called the children "simple monstrosities".

[16] Northern Whig — 27 October 1853, p.3.

[17] Dickens, C. (1853) Household Words Volume VII. p.574. – "…every actor in the story was conveniently packed out of the world before the exhibition opened. Velasquez himself — having, we suppose, disposed of his interest in the children — seems to have retired into the clouds. Our belief is that he never did himself consist of anything much more substantial.

"No confection can be coarser than the assumed journal of Velasquez. The writer has incessantly the exhibition-room before him, and is assuming candour, and forestalling objections to his tale among the audience. What can be more intensely ridiculous than this picture of the man of business, who has been bitten with enthusiasm for the discovery of the mysterious city, sitting on the top of a mountain some ten thousand feet high, pencil in hand; and, while the first view of the city is obtained, keeping a running comment in his diary …"

[18] Ibid. p.576.

[19] Ibid.

[20] Ibid.

[21] Ibid.

[22] Ibid.

[23] London Standard — 12 July 1853, p.1.

[24] Owen had casts made of the children's teeth, which are still in the Hunterian Museum at the Royal College of Surgeons, Odontological Collection. See Dental casts of the Extraordinary Aztec Children, 1853 — http://morbidanatomy.blogspot.co.uk/2014/07/dental-casts-of-extraordinary-aztec.html (last accessed 13 July 2015).

[25] Ibid. 3.

[26] Manchester Times — 18 March 1854, p.4.

[27] Manchester Courier and Lancashire General Advertiser — 08 April 1854, p.9. – "THE AZTECS. — PRESENTATION TO MR. ROBERT DIBB. – A testimonial encased in morocco, and lined with blue satin, has been presented to Mr. Robert Dibb by Mr. Morris, the guardian of the Lilliputians, for the kindness and attention shown to the Aztec Lilliputians during their successful visits through schools in Manchester. The number of schools in Manchester and the suburbs visited by the Aztecs were 125, and the Sunday and day scholars who saw them were 37,000, one school alone (Bennett-street) numbering 1,200." – Robert Dibb was a theatrical and exhibition agent in Manchester.

[28] Ibid. 26.

[29] Illustrated London News — 6 November 1852, p.371.

[30] Ibid.

[31] Morning Post — 6 May 1853, p.1.

[32] Ibid. 23. — 9 May 1853, p.4. – The Illustrated London News (Ibid. 28.) tells us, "Both children have an excellent ear for music, and sing the 'Buffalo Gals,' 'I'm going to Alabama,' and 'Britons never shall be Slaves,' with evident enjoyment. They also dance together, and Flora, being entreated to dance a schottische, moves about with the easy and natural grace peculiar to her sex."

[33] Ibid. — 14 September 1853, p.2. "CREMORNE — Admission, 1s — Thursday Sept. 15. — T.B. SIMPSON, in announcing another EXTRA DAY and NIGHT FETE … will embrace the novel and highly interesting exhibitions of the Zulu Kafirs, the extraordinary Aztec Lilliputians, and the highly interesting and talented Earth Children, which, together will form an extraordinary and rare ethological group …"

[34] The Times — 7 May 1853, p.5.

[35] Morning Chronicle — 23 September 1854, p.3.

[36] Conolly, J. (1854) The Ethnological Exhibitions Of London. p.28-29.

[37] Liverpool Mercury — 23 March 1864, p.1.

[38] Morning Post — 8 January 1867, p.3.

[39] The Era — 29 June 1879, p.3.

[40] Bogdan, R. (1988) Freak Show: Presenting Human Oddities for Amusement and Profit, p.131-132.

[41] For a full biography of Schlitze see http://www.imdb.com/name/nm0772396/bio (last accessed 17 July 2015).

[42] For example, King, E.F. (1st Edition 1859, continued to be published at least until 1889) Ten Thousand Wonderful Things Comprising The Marvellous And Rare, Odd, Curious, Quaint Eccentric And Extraordinary In All Ages And Nations, In Art, Nature, And Science Including Many Wonders Of The-World includes a chapter on the children. Subscribers to this book included Jane Austen's and Lewis Carroll's families (see essay, Gregory, J. Eccentric lives: Character, character and curiosities in Britain, c.1760-1900 n.55. in Ernst, W. (Ed) (2006) Histories of the Normal and Abnormal, Social and Cultural Histories of Norms and Normativity).

[43] Popular Mechanics — Aug 1926, p.270. – "For many years there have been rumours in Yucatan that somewhere in the interior of the jungle there still exists a city, called Iximaya, inhabited by the last remnants of the powerful Mayas, but no one has ever seen it, and come back to tell the tale. Two Americans who went in search of the city several years ago never returned. The native rumours, however, describe the city as being surrounded by a wall four miles in length, inclosing vast temples and altars to the sun."

Arthur Nelson and Popular Entertainment 1840 – 1860

Nelson's interlude providing musical accompaniment for other acts was out of the ordinary in a career that spanned two decades. In the autumn of 1859 he returned to the circus, appearing at McCollum's Great Anglo Saxon Circus, Royal Alhambra Palace, Leicester Square[1]. The London Standard's review of the performance stated:

"We believe, however, that we are correct in stating that no portion of the evening's amusement gave more satisfaction than Mr. Arthur Nelson's (one of the clowns) musical selections on the wood and rock harmonicons. In the execution of the various airs played by Mr. Arthur Nelson he displayed an extraordinary taste, and satisfied us that he possesses a most correct knowledge of the ordinary mysteries of music. The variations which he superadded to the airs astonished the audience, who loudly encored his efforts. The tones brought out from the materials with which he had to deal were marvellously good, and we hope, for the sake of those who frequent the Alhambra, that Mr. Nelson will continue his musical efforts in this peculiar department.[2]"

Arthur Nelson was more than a musical novelty act. In 1855, he had "invented, arranged and produced" the "bold achievement and progress of the Siege of Sebastopol" for E.T. Smith's Mammoth Circus[3] — "In order to give due effect to the various Tableaux, the entire of the Drury Lane Equestrian Troupe: the splendid Stud of Horses and high-couraged chargers, the costly military trappings, appliances and appointments, and upwards of Fifty auxiliaries, together with Batteries of 500 Guns, will be brought into requisition to carry out the great and glorious effect[4]".

It was perhaps during this tour that Nelson learnt of 'the Dunmow flitch of Bacon' as E.T. Smith had been intimately involved in the revival of this event in 1855[5].

This ancient custom involved the awarding of a flitch of bacon to any couple that could swear that they had not, during the last year and a day, had a quarrel or, for one moment, regretted their marriage. Although, this custom had existed in different parts of the country, the ceremony in Little Dunmow in Essex was the best known, having been referred to by Chaucer in the Wife of Bath's tale[6]. The couple were required to kneel on sharp stones in the churchyard while taking the oath:

"You shall swear by custom of confession,
That you ne'er made nuptial transgression;
Nor, since you were married man and wife,
By household brawls, or contentious strife,
Or otherwise at bed or board,
Offended each other in deed or in word,
Or since the parish clerk said, Amen,
Wished yourselves unmarried again,
Or in twelvemonth and a day,
Repented in thought any way,
But continue true in thought and desire,
As when you joined hands in holy quire.
If to these conditions without all fear,
Of your own accord you will freely swear,
A whole gammon of bacon you shall receive,
And bear it hence with love and good leave:
For this is our custom at Dunmow well known,
Tho' the pleasure be ours, the bacon's your own.[7]"

THE DUNMOW PROCESSION, JUNE 20, 1751, FROM A
PRINT OF THE TIME, BY DAVID OGBORNE
Illustrated London News 28 July 1855, p.108.

The couple were then paraded around the village on a chair to loud cheering. While no award of the flitch had been made since 1751, the tradition had been turned into a comic opera in 1780 by Henry Bale and became the basis of a popular novel by William Harrison Ainsworth in 1854[8]. Indeed, the revival of the event in 1855 was a marketing ploy by Ainsworth. Ainsworth would donate two flitches and be master of ceremonies, and E.T. Smith would organise the parade and fête in conjunction with the visit of his circus to the town. This modern version involved a jury who would decide the couple's case[9].

Nelson was to use this story, together with music from Bale's comic opera, as the basis of a spectacular ending for the show at the Alhambra in 1859:

"The attractive equestrian performances of Mr. McCollum's grand cirque classique have this week been rendered additionally effective by the production of a spectacular illustration of the old English custom of the Flitch of Bacon being claimed at Dunmow in 1751, a subject well suited to amphitheatrical displays. The spectacle has been cleverly arranged by Mr. Arthur Nelson, from the descriptions of the old ceremony given in Harrison Ainsworth's novel, and the action is appropriately accompanied by selections from the Rev. Henry Bale's comic opera of The Flitch of Bacon, produced eighty years ago at the old Haymarket, and for which Shield composed some lively characteristic music. Opening with a grand procession of horse and foot, and introducing, on what may be supposed to represent the village-green, the principal rural sports and pastimes with which our forefathers celebrated every festival, the whole of the equestrian company is very effectively employed. Wrestling, quarter-staff fighting, single-stick, and the mummers' sword-play, are practised in succession with a fidelity to the ancient usages of such rough games as would have delighted the heart of Strutt to have seen so accurately illustrated from his authority. Morris dances and the spirit-stirring 'Sir Roger de Coverley' give additional animation to the scene, and the happy couple receive the prize awarded to them for their endurance of their conjugal fidelity amidst such chairing and cheering as Dunmow itself might have witnessed a hundred years ago. All this, pleasantly wrought out with evident care, and brought out with commendable liberality, forms a pleasingly characteristic tableau at the close of the performances, which will add much to the gratification of the visitors.[10]"

By November Nelson had taken an engagement in Birmingham where Wallett, the clown, was managing the Royal Alhambra Palace Circus in Moor Street. He received top billing with Wallett himself:

"ROYAL ALHAMBRA PALACE CIRCUS,
MOOR STREET, BIRMINGHAM.

———

GRAND CHANGE OF PERFORMANCES AND PERFORMERS.
DURING THE SHOW WEEK,
A DAY EXHIBITION EVERY AFTERNOON,
At half past Two, by Gas-light.
GO SEE THE THOUSAND GUINEA CHANDELIER.
THIS PRESENT MONDAY, November the 28th, first appearance of the
world-wide known Wit, Wag, and Clown,
ARTHUR NELSON,
who will appear each Exhibition, and electrify the audience by the flagues
of his wit, or melt and subdue their hearts with the soul-stirring music of
his
ROCK HARMONICON.
RE-APPEARANCE OF WALLETT, THE JESTER.
NEW SCENES, NEW COMPANY.
Open every evening at Seven o'clock, commence at half past Seven.[11]"

He was to remain there until Christmas, and in the new year found himself once again in Edinburgh at Sangers' Monstre Circus and Hippodrome in Nicholson Street. The vogue in 1860 was for horse taming, and Sanger's circus had also engaged John Rarey, an American, who provided demonstrations in the circus ring having invited the audience beforehand to bring unruly and abused horses so they could be tamed by him. In one short English tour in 1858, it was said he earned £25,000:

"The horse tamer skips into the Circus with a sort of springy high walk and half trot, like a man who is accustomed to being 'in the straw,' and has acquired this style of locomotion to keep his legs clear of any incumbrance. Giving a bow and a kind of polka kick round to the company, he delivered a few introductory words (which will be found amplified in his sixpenny book) on his experience and mode of treatment, and his practice of appealing to the good sense and intelligence rather than the fear of the horse. You see at once he is an uneducated, but original, shrewd, and observing man. His face too is firm and resolute without being at all fierce; on the contrary, the good forehead, fair complexion, clear grey eye, light hair and regular aquiline features, prepossess you in his favour as a man with plenty of pluck and a frank and friendly nature. He is about thirty-three years old, of the middle size, and a well formed wiry figure. After speaking of himself and his system, he referred to his four-legged travelling companion 'Cruiser,' who by this time had sufficiently filled the 'trump of fame' not to require an elaborate introduction to the English public. Suffice to say, 'Cruiser,' a high-bred sire, was the property of Lord Dorchester, but now belongs to the Ohio Tamer, who uses him to some purpose and profit as a 'horrid example' in all his expositions. He was as bad as any horse could be, and I believe is

THE SUPPOSED INCURABLE HORSE "CRUISER" UNDER MR
RAREY'S TREATMENT. — DRAWN BY JOHN LEECH.
Illustrated London News 24 April 1858, p.413.

not even now fully trusted out of his Yankee master's hands.[12]"

Arthur Nelson's last performance in London was at the Alhambra Palace in April where he introduced Miss. Ashton, an eighteen year old "farmer's daughter", as "the only female horse tamer who has appeared in public[13]".

Nelson was to spend the summer touring season of 1860 with Pablo Fanque's Circus, despite the proprietor having been made bankrupt in February of that year. The tour was of the industrial midland towns of Lancashire and Yorkshire with working class audiences looking for entertainment on a summer's evening. However, regardless of a varied troupe, including six clowns, audiences were disappointing, as the Burnley Advertiser pointed out:

"PABLO FANQUE'S CIRCUS — During the week, the old favourite, Pablo Fanque, has been giving his celebrated performances in a large and commodious circus tent on a plot of ground at Fulledge. Two entertainments each day have generally been given, rather too often we think, when the stay is over one day, as may be judged from the fact of very poor attendance up to the last night. We are very sorry Mr. Pablo has overlooked this. For as far as the performances go they can not be equalled, the different artistes have been carefully selected, the majority of their feats are good and original, and elicited 'thunders of applause.' Mr.

ASTLEY'S. — MR. PABLO FANQUE, AND HIS TRAINED STEED
Illustrated London News 20 March 1847, p.189.

149

Pablo introduced his wonderful and beautiful mare, 'Miss Nightingale or Lady Ayr,' her performances are truly unprecedented. Six clowns contributed greatly to the fun of the entertainment. Last night was under the patronage of Capt. Dugdale and the officers and members of the Burnley Rifle Corps. The corps mustered in uniform at Keighley Green and headed by the band proceeded to the circus. We earnestly wish Mr. Pablo success.[14]"

The same was true the following week at Colne, which was in the midst of a hand-loom weaver strike:

"PABLO'S CIRCUS. — On Wednesday and Thursday this circus visited Colne, and gave three performances. We are sorry Mr. Pablo Fanque has not met with that success which he usually has done here, but probably this may be attributed to the strike, and the very gloomy aspect of things are at present assuming. We can however recommend a visit by anyone, and we feel assured they will not regret doing so, Mr. Pablo's present company being decidedly superior to any which has visited Colne for some time.[15]"

It is extremely doubtful whether Arthur Nelson was with the troupe at Colne, as he was to die at his lodging house in Brunswick Road, Burnley of 'mortification of the lower extremities' on 27 July. The circumstances of his death from gangrene are unknown. No evidence of an accident is recorded in the press, but the infection of a small wound or crushing of a foot or leg could have been the cause. Given Nelson's schedule over the past year, although there are some months when no record of him working can be found, it is unlikely that this was the result of a long term affliction.

Arthur Nelson was buried on 31 July 1860 in Burnley cemetery. Pablo Fanque placed a rather poignant, if not mysterious, advertisement in the Era the following month:

"MR. A.M. NELSON died at Burnley, July 27th, 1860 and was interred at the Burnley Cemetery, July 31st, followed by Pablo Fanque and a few more friends. The little property which he had when he died, such as dulcimer sticks and rocks; his clothes, and Clown's dresses, are now lying at Mr. Bentley's, Bill-poster, Bradford. His friends can have them if they drop a letter directed to Pablo Fanque, at Mr. Bentley's, when things will

ARTHUR NELSON'S GRAVESTONE, BURNLEY CEMETERY
PLOT 7814
(June 2015)

be explained to them. Not necessary to be published here.[16]"

His wife registered his death, so it would seem that the family were not interested in his possessions.

Arthur Nelson's career (1840-1860) provides an opportunity to explore popular entertainment and how it related to the culture of the period. Entertainment developed alongside the industrial revolution both in Britain and America, from the penny-gaff and fair culture of the theatrical booth, to the theatrical pantomime and equestrian circus. The latter, being mostly unaffordable to the working classes in the 1840s, became a mainstay of popular entertainment during the 1850s, particularly following the transatlantic boom of American tented circuses. These transformed the form and nature of the circus, and although permanent buildings, as well as temporary wooden circus amphitheatres, continued well into the second half of the nineteenth century, they did begin to slowly diminish in number. While circuses still revolved around equestrianism, by 1860 animals such as elephants, tigers and other exotic animals from menageries accompanying circuses on their tours, were being integrated into performances in the ring. Such performances involved the animal cages being towed into the ring in which the 'tamers' would conduct their highly dangerous acts. The greatest exponents of this trend were George and John Sanger, who built one of the largest circuses in the second half of the nineteenth century[17]. The combination of animal acts with circus performance was perhaps an indication that audiences were no longer just content with the skill and daring of the equestrian; the introduction of exotic animals added additional danger and spice to the show. Such adaptations meant that theatres and even multipurpose buildings, such as the Alhambra Palace; were also losing their circus rings[18]. The mainstay of circus performance however remained the same: equestrianism, acrobats and rope walking, and clowning. The fact that these had limited variations meant that performers who could provide something unique thrived. Nelson's 'musical novelty' ensured that he almost invariably could find circus work, but also enabled him to provide idiosyncratic entertainment in theatrical pantomime and accompaniment for distinctive acts such as tableau vivant and the Aztec Lilliputians. In addition, he could hold his own in concert halls with other comic performers such as William Harrison.

While Nelson's specialism was a key attribute to his success, either as a musician or as a clown, it is the combination of the two that makes his career unique. 'Talking' or Shakespearean clowns of the period were required to ensure their material was up to date, relevant and funny. Their jokes (wheezes), monologues and dialogue brought the real world into the make-believe spectacle of the circus ring or theatrical pantomime. As Nelson himself said in an advertisement in February 1858, "Mr. N. boldly and justly asserts, that for quantity, quality, originality and variety, he has no compeer. Having disposed of his old stock of jokes to other clowns, is in himself a new man and Model Joseph.[19]".

In the first half of Victoria's reign the clown had come to mean a particular type of comedian. Whether it be through physical comedic acts such as slapstick, or wit and repartee, the clown could take liberties on stage or in the circus ring that others could not. This irreverence might sometimes be seen as a danger to social convention if it spilt over into the real world. This can be illustrated by one incident in Nottingham in October 1857. Nelson had brought a charge of neglect of duty and improper conduct against detective Bacon of the Nottingham police force. On Sunday 18 October while walking back to his lodgings in Nottingham, Nelson and another circus performer called Armstrong had found a man in the street. When they realised he was seriously injured they called the police. Nelson's reported evidence stated:

"Bacon came up, and inquired what all that row was about, and he (complainant) [Nelson] and his friend told him and another officer, who were going to leave the man in the street, that if he died there his death would lay at his door. They then began abusing witness, telling him that he was only a common showman — nothing but a clown, and that they wanted none of his acting, nor clowning there; he was not in the circus then. Bacon told him he would knock his d—d head through the wall, and would lock him up. Mr. Armstrong collaborated Mr. Nelson's statement. — In defence Bacon said that at the time in question he was in the company of Inspector Gilbert, and, hearing a cry of 'watch,' they went to the place whence proceeded, and there found a man on the ground, and at first thought he was dead. ... Mr Nelson said to them after they had raised the man, 'Why, you're going to leave him, and if he dies his death will lie at your door.' They told him they were not going to leave him, and Inspector Gilbert said, 'We do not want any of your spouting here, as they do in the circus.' Nelson then began abusing them, and calling them, 'the scum of the earth' — Inspector Gilbert gave similar testimony, stating that Nelson said he would not be humbugged by them, but would see that the man had shelter. He also stated that Nelson had had drink, which statement was confirmed by a young man named Wynn. The Inspector said Nelson put his fist in Bacon's face, which caused him to say he would knock his head against the wall.[20]"

Needless to say, the case was dismissed, but the comments of the police officers provide an insight into authority's attitude towards the profession of 'clown' within society. Indeed, the police, as figures of the establishment, were, in turn, easy pickings and often the butt of jokes and songs by clowns in their performances[21].

As we have already discovered the clown's standing in the theatre and pantomime was also regarded as suspect. His special relationship with the audience meant it was not necessary for him to be a 'team player' among the others on stage and his role could be regarded as secondary to the main purpose of the plot. He could be a loose cannon, reacting to the mood of the audience, which made his actions unpredictable in the drama. Nelson's incident with Frederick Neale, the stage manager at the Pavilion in 1851, may not just have been an indication of personal feelings running high, but could highlight the way in which clowns in general were viewed with suspicion within the professional community.

Popular entertainment also reflected many paradoxes in early Victorian society. In this period, theories of racial superiority had not developed and Britain and popular opinion supported the abolition of slavery in the 1830s. Men and women who were not Caucasian white were readily accepted by audiences in the entertainment industries and applauded for their skills, yet few spoke out about the exhibition and display of human beings as morally indefensible. Such exhibitions were easily justifiable to their middle class audiences as culturally educational and of scientific interest, a fact ruthlessly exploited by some showmen of the period. This distinction was also made in reference to the display of semi-naked bodies for the sake of art, as the reporter for the Leicester Mercury pointed out in reviewing Professor Keller's exhibition of Pose Plastiques and Tableau Vivants in 1846:

"During the exhibition, we felt at times slightly suggestive; but our temerity was instantly checked by the overwhelming impression of its high excellence.[22]"

The use of working children was routine in Victorian society and there would have been no moral distinction between those that worked in the entertainment industry than in other occupations. Those that were brought up to perform were apprentices, often with better expectations that those who might become skilled artisans. When Martinis and Flora were taught to sing, dance and play the pianoforte their earning potential in adult life was good.

The cross-fertilisation of entertainment culture from both sides of the Atlantic is all too evident when one looks at the acts that populated the concert halls, theatres, and eventually circuses, in Britain and the eastern cities of the United States. Not only were blackface singers and minstrels readily making the trip across the water, but also their songs became as much part of the regular fare for entertainers as traditional English ballads. The Vauxhall Song Book, published in 1847 by John W. Sharp, the Musical Director of the Vauxhall Gardens, is dominated by such songs as 'Buffalo Gals', 'Coal Black Rose', 'Dere's Somebody in de House wid Dinah' and 'Zip Coon' alongside 'Where are you going, my pretty Maid' and 'Tommy Tadpole's Courtship'.

Rapid economic and social change meant that audiences were readily available and entertainers were able to move quickly from one engagement to another through an efficient transport system, whether by rail within the United Kingdom, or by sea across the Atlantic. A typical engagement contract meant that the proprietor or manager could send the entertainer anywhere during the period of their employment[23]. This added to the strain on itinerate performers, who might move from one venue to another in relatively quick succession as theatre managers and circus proprietors needed to change their acts repeatedly in order to fill their seats. For those working in the circus, the increase in 'tenting' compounded the workload. James Cooke's visit to Stirling at the end of the 1854 season sums up the nature of the business:

"COOKE'S CIRCUS.—On Monday last the celebrated equestrian company of Mr James Cooke visited Stirling on their way to Glasgow. They made a grand entree, into the town little before noon, and after parading some of the principal streets, put up at the Golden Lion Hotel. The procession was headed by a char-a-banc carrying the band, and was drawn by eight richly caparisoned horses, driven and managed by Mr. Cooke himself. This was followed by other vehicles, and by a number of riders, male and female, whose sporting habits, flowing down the sides of their piebald steeds gave the affair a sufficient degree of variety. A young lady who visited the circus in the evening was over heard to say that 'the people and the horses delighted in horribly eccentric colours' — a rather eccentric expression from a young lady. They erected a large marquee in a park at the foot of Craigs, and gave two performances, the first commencing at 2, and the second at 7 o'clock p.m. The attendances were numerous. The equestrians performed their feats with astonishing dexterity. The gymnastics were perfectly incredible, few we dare say will be prepared to admit, if they did not see it, that a man could climb to the top of a pole forty or fifty feet long, held up by another. Yet this was done with all ease. The holder of the pole placed the end of it on his breast, and with both his hands held it upright, while the other scrambled to the top and performed some curious gyrations. The clowns were as usual full of fun and repartee. The concluding part of the performances was entitled the 'Barber's Shop,' which was altogether a laughable affair. Two wights who stepped in for a shave were lathered out of a bucket till their heads seemed a huge lump of soap suds. The razor was about six feet long, and was useful for other purposes than shaving. We cannot help thinking that the clowns were hard enough on the ladies. For example the following atrocious joke was perpetrated their expense: 'How are ladies more troubled with the toothache than men? Because their tongues go so much and so fast that they wear off the enamel of the teeth.' Again, Harlequin, in illustrating his pedestrian powers, said he once walked into the affections of a young lady, and almost married her, but was stopt, — because she would not have him. Before the audience was wholly dispersed, the frame work of the tent was almost entirely stript of its covering, and in the course an hour or two afterwards, the whole would be bundled and on its way to Balfron where they were perform on Tuesday and thence to Glasgow, to take up their winter quarters.[24]"

Unlike Richard Flexmore[25], who died a month later, friends and fellow artistes of his generation did not feel moved to contribute to a monument to Arthur Nelson. He had no time, leisure or 'retirement' to set out his claims through stories of success like 'Lord' George Sanger[26]; nor did he have the opportunity of justify his actions or glorify his place in circus history like William Wallett[27]. However, it can be argued that Arthur Nelson's diverse career provides an interesting and rare insight into the culture of popular entertainment and its expansion in the early Victorian period.

---

[1] Bell's Life in London and Sporting Chronicle — 11 September 1859, p.2.

[2] London Evening Standard — 15 October 1859, p.6.

[3] Oxford University and City Herald — 7 July 1855, p.16.

[4] Hertford Mercury and Reformer — 14 July 1855, p.1.

[5] The Era —24 June 1855, p.9. – "Mr. E. T. Smith respectfully announces to the nobility, gentry, and public desirous of information respecting the flitches of bacon to be given away according to ancient custom … 300 tickets only will be issued for the Town Hall, which can be had from Mr. Smith, at Drury-lane Theatre, and tickets for the enclosed meadow, where the fête will be held, can be had from Mr. Charles Pavey, at Dunmow, and also of Mr. Smith. … Arrangements will be made with the Eastern Counties Railway for the conveyance of visitors desirous of going and returning the same day."

[6] "The bacon was nat fet for hem, I trowe, / That som men han in Essex at Dunmowe." — The Wife of Bath's Prologue and Tale, see http://sites.fas.harvard.edu/~chaucer/teachslf/wbt-par.htm, lines 217–18.

[7] Percy, S. and Percy, R. (1826) The Percy Anecdotes, Original and Select Volume XII. P.177-178.

[8] Ainsworth, W. H. (1854) The Flitch of Bacon – The Custom of Dunmow: a tale of English Home – The story revolves around the scheming of the leading character to be awarded the flitch by marrying a succession of women.

[9] The revived custom is still performed today on every leap year at Great Dunmow, see http://www.dunmowflitchtrials.co.uk/

[10] Ibid. 5. — 23 October 1859, p.15.

[11] Aris's Birmingham Gazette — 28 November 1859, p.3.

[12] Exeter Flying Post — 5 January 1860, p.6. quoted from Bristol Times.

[13] Newcastle Guardian and Tyne Mercury — 21 April 1860, p.6. – "The extraordinary young lady gave an exposition of her extraordinary nerve and talent in the subjugation of unbroken colts at the Alhambra Palace last week, and notwithstanding the short time allowed for its announcement there was a numerous and highly respectable audience. The charges were a guinea for reserved seats, half a guinea, second seats. This was her first appearance in public, and she was introduced by Mr. Arthur Nelson, who made a few preliminary remarks with his usual ability."

[14] Burnley Advertiser — 14 July 1860, p.3.

[15] Ibid. — 21 July 1860, p.3.

[16] Ibid. 5. — 19 August 1860, p.1. – Pablo Fanque's circus had arrived in Bradford on 1 August.

[17] Manchester Courier and Lancashire General Advertiser — 9 March 1861, p.1. – "A GRAND WEEK OF NOVELTIES, SANGAR'S CIRCUS, THE LION KING. MR. JAMES CROOKETT, will introduce the Noble Troupe of PERFORMING LIONS. This Evening, and during the week. Go see, and believe!!!"

[18] Lloyd's Weekly Newspaper — 30 September 1860, p.7. – "THE ALHAMBRA PALACE, after many roving years – dissolving views, scientific lectures, organs, coloured fountains, &c. the sports of the American circus, clowns, bull fights and balloons; after the ridiculous farce of Sayers and Heenan, and a fresh turn at horse racing – the Alhambra-palace, we hear will now be devoted to music." (Sayers and Heenan refers to the first international boxing championship fight between Tom Sayers and John C. Heenan. The illegal contest in a field near Farnborough was a draw. Both men were to die before the age of 40.)

[19] Ibid. 5. — 14 February 1858, p.1.

[20] Nottinghamshire Guardian — 29 October 1857, p.3.

[21] Many examples of this can be found in Bratton, J. and Featherstone, A. (2006) The Victorian Clown which reproduces the 1871 gagbook of Thomas Lawrence. Here is one example:
"Did you ever see my brother Bill — he was a policeman.
I shall never forget the last time I saw him.
I went into his room, his feet were fast to the ground.
His face was buried in his hands, the tears came trickling down
And with one despairing yell from his soul he cries —
I can't find the towel, and the soap's got in my eyes.", p.184.

[22] Leicestershire Mercury — 30 May 1846, p.3.

[23] The Era — 18 December 1859, p.10. – a typical contract of engagement can be seen in the court case between William Wallett and an acrobat in 1859:
"AGREEMENT:
Agreement between William Fredrick Wallett, on the one part and Assam Ben Mahommed, on the other part. W. F. W. agrees to pay £6 per week for services for the space of six months, from the 24th of April to the end of September, 1859. Assam agrees to play whensoever and wheresoever Mr. Wallett directs, in England, Ireland, Scotland, or Wales, on consideration of his passage and transit money being paid by Mr. Wallett. He further agrees not to give his name, lithographs, or woodcuts for any other establishment, without consent, or forfeit £50.
(Signed) W. F. WALLETT / ASSAM BEN MOHOMMED
(Witness) JOHN ORNE."

[24] Stirling Observer — 28 September 1854, p.3.

[25] Ibid 5. — 9 February 1862, p.11 – "THE FLEXMORE MONUMENT. …
The Monument consists of a double plinth, surmounting a noble pedestal has, on
the angles, four masked-heads, representing Tragedy and Comedy on one side,
and Music and Poetry on the other, suspending on the four sides festoons
composed of oak and ivy leaves bound with ribbon, fancy slippers, with an Urn
entwined with a laurel wreath. The height of the whole monument, complete, is
nine feet six inches. The design, furnished by Mr. Richard Wynn Keene, an artist
so familiar to the public under his punning pseudonym of Dykewynken, has
been ably executed by Mr. John Chapman, Sculptor, 23, East-place, Walworth.
The following is the inscription: —

In Memory of
RICHARD FLEXMORE GATTER,
Who died August 20th, 1860

———

'A fellow on infinite jest.' — SHAKSPERE

———

This Tribute, in estimation of Worthiness and Talent,
Is Erected by Sincere Friends and Fellow Artists."

[26] Sanger G. (1908) Seventy Years a Showman.

[27] Luntley J, ed. (1870) The Public Life of W. F. W., the Queen's Jester: an
Autobiography see https://books.google.co.uk/books?id=MaZcAAAAcAAJ&pg
(last assessed 30 July 2015).

Appendix — Nelson's Musical Instruments

Arthur Nelson's appeal lay in the fact that he was more than a 'talking clown' he was also an excellent musician. The reason his performances are well documented in newspaper reports is the very fact that he stood out. While other clowns of the period got a passing sentence, his performances were noteworthy.

The Dulcimer

The least unusual of Nelson's instruments was the dulcimer, a percussion and stringed instrument in which the strings are stretched over a trapezoidal sounding board. It is usually mounted on a stand at an angle, and the musician strikes the strings with small mallets. The critic on the Boston Musical Gazette described Nelson's instrument in 1846:

"In form, it resembles the octochord represented in our last number. Its compass appeared to be about two octaves. Some of the tones are produced by four strings struck together, others by two, and others by three. It is played with small, leather-covered mallets, held in the performer's hands, i.e., the strings are struck like the strings of a piano, with the difference, that the dulcimer player holds the hammer in his hand. We did not have an opportunity to satisfy ourself whether or not David performed on a precisely similar instrument. We can only say that if he did, and could make his mallets fly like the performer on the present occasion, the modern school of execution, as it is called, is not so new by two or three thousand years as we had supposed.[1]"

The Pine Sticks

The musical pine sticks were a type of xylophone, probably constructed by Nelson himself:

"'The Musical Sticks, are nothing more nor less, than sixteen pine sticks, (take notice ye who live where timber's plenty,) about an inch square, and somewhere from one to three feet long, laid upon ropes of straw, and played upon with wooden hammers, producing the richest melody.' The quotation is from the performers' advertisement. We can hardly admit that there is so much melody in them, as we have heard produced from some other things; but we will confess there is a hundred times more than we ever dreamed could lie concealed in rough pine chips. If excellence in instrumental performance consists in rapid playing, then Mr. Nelson is a magnificent 'Pine Stickist'. If his drum sticks didn't go it, then Ole Bull's elbows never did.[2]"

The Rock Harmonicon

This instrument was perhaps the most noticed by the audience and commentators alike. Although Nelson claimed he had invented the 'rock harmonicon', there were two other purer claimants to its origin. The first was Joseph Richardson[3], a Cumbrian mason, who said that he had spent thirteen years perfecting the instrument. Touring Britain in 1841, it was played by his three sons:

"Those who are acquainted with the toy harmonicon, pieces of glass laid on tapes to be struck with the cork-hammer, will readily form an idea of Mr. Richardson's instrument. In his, however, the sonorous material is mica schist from Skiddaw, or, as it is known in Cumberland and generally, whinstone. He found it the best suited for his purpose. Slabs varying in length from about three feet to five inches, of about three inches wide, and one and a half thick, are placed on an extensive hollow frame with two ridges gradually approaching each other; the ridges whereon the stones rest are covered with strips of cloth, and on them straw bands run the whole length. They comprise five octaves and a half, with all the additional semitones. What perseverance must have been exercised to produce the shape and size for each differing note: The blows are given with wooden hammers, small and of lignum vitae for the treble, larger and of softer wood for the middle notes, and larger still and covered with leather for the base. For the centre keys sometimes are used hammers, with two knobs on each, in the form of a crutch handle to strike thirds. The Rock Harmonicon is played by the three sons of the inventor, and the slightest, softest touch causes the sullen slate to sound, and so sweetly But it must be heard to be appreciated.[4]"

Another Cumbrian, Mr. Bowe, also claimed he had invented the rock harmonicon about the same time, and together with a Mr. Graves undertook concerts in the north of England using the instrument, played by three hired musicians[5].

Certainly, Nelson's rock harmonicon was simpler in nature, having to be much more portable and with no more than himself as musician. The same critic at the Boston Musical Gazette, taking his cue from Nelson's advertisement described it as:

"… an instrument 'composed of forty rough pieces of stone, from the celebrated Skiddaw mountains, Cumberland, England — laid loosely on straw covered slats, and played upon with small wooden mallets, producing the most exquisite music, surpassing the piano and musical glasses blended.' The tones produced from the stones, were good, although a slightly unpleasant sensation is produced upon the ear, from the fact, perhaps, that they cannot be so nicely tuned, as a violin or pianoforte.[6]"

Although Nelson displayed his musical talent on these instruments he was also an improviser, whether it be the objects he played, or in the way they were described. He realised that audiences were enchanted by the fact that he could make music out of ordinary objects, hence his advertisement to Australian Managers in which he stated he was a "Performer on the Monstre Dolcimello, Rock Harmonicon, Musical Pine Sticks, Steel Bars, China Plates, Musical Glasses and Clay Pantiles[7]". In an advertisement for McCollum's Great Anglo-Saxon Circus in 1859, he claimed he was the "Inventor and Performer on the Lignum Phonicon, Improver of the Ancient Dulcimer and Lyre[8]" and while taking on the persona of an American clown he was quick to rebrand his rocks as 'Niagara Stones'.

In summing up Nelson's musical performances we can do no better than quote that Boston critic's final remarks:

"When we attend an exhibition of musical novelty, or an exhibition for the display of feats of execution, we go with the same kind of feelings with which we go to witness any other curious performance. On the score of what we call music, Mr. Nelson's harmonican would hardly compare with that heard from a well-trained orchestra, nor do his pine sticks rank very high with regard to tone; still they are curiosities well worth seeing. Rocks and trees here literally break forth into singing. On the score of execution, we do not see why Mr. N. does not rank with the most rapid pianoforte players and violinists who have been among us. Some of the movements performed on the rock harmonican, were in as quick time as one often hears on any instrument. Considering that he has but two fingers (mallets,) where pianists can use ten, and also that he has to strike stones extending over a large surface, the rapidity with which he 'hits' right and left, is perfectly astonishing. Viewing, as we do, the merits of those artists who have had such crowds to witness their wonderful 'skill,' who can blame us for predicting for the scientific performer on the 'sticks and stones,' full houses, showers of silver, and may-hap a wreath or two of flowers!!!⁹"

---

[1] The Boston Musical Gazette — 30 January 1846.

[2] Ibid.

[3] Richardson's Rock Harmonicon can still be seen today in the Keswick Museum and Art Gallery see http://keswickmuseum.org.uk/

[4] The Literary Gazette and Journal of the Belle Lettres, Arts, Sciences &c. — 26 June 1841, p.414.

[5] Carlisle Journal —24 April 1841, p.3. – "Rock Harmonicon.— Some sensation has been created amongst the musical public here, the arrival of Messrs. Bowe and Graves, of Keswick, with their Rock Harmonicon. The name gives little idea of the nature of the instrument, if 'instrument' it may be called. It consists of about fifty stones, in the rude unhewn state in which they have been taken, after immense labour, from the side of the mountain and in the quarries of Skiddaw. The stones are placed upon a sort of sounding board, and played upon three men, with small wooden hammers; and almost any air may be played upon them —the brilliancy of tone and perfect harmony produced being delightful as they are wonderful. We assure our readers that a visit to the Rock Harmonicon will afford a treat of no ordinary kind."

[6] Ibid. 1.

[7] The Era — 27 August 1854, p.1.

[8] Morning Chronicle — 12 September 1859, p.1.

[9] Ibid. 1.

Illustrations

Every effort has been made to trace copyright holders. Any that have been overlooked are invited to get in touch via www.theclownking.com.

Bibliography

Ainsworth, W. H. (1854) The Flitch of Bacon – The Custom of Dunmow: a tale of English Home.

Anon. (1762) A Description of VAUX-HALL GARDENS Being A proper companion and guide for all who visit that place.

Anon. (1853) Illustrated Memoir of the Eventful Expedition into Central America Resulting in the Discovery of the Idolatrous City of Iximaya, in an Unexplored Region.

Barber, C. (pub) (1846) Guide to Great Yarmouth with Thirty-four Illustrations by Brooke Utting.

Bogdan, R. (1988) Freak Show: Presenting Human Oddities for Amusement and Profit.

Booth, M. (1991) Theatre in the Victorian Age.

Bratton, J. and Featherstone, A. (2006) The Victorian Clown.

Davies, G. H. H. (2015) The Fall of Yarmouth Suspension Bridge: A Norfolk Disaster.

Dickens, C. (1853) Household Words Volume VII.

Ernst, W. (Ed) (2006) Histories of the Normal and Abnormal, Social and Cultural Histories of Norms and Normativity.

Kennedy, D. (2010) The Oxford Companion to Theatre and Performance.

King, E. F. (1859) Ten Thousand Wonderful Things Comprising The Marvellous And Rare, Odd, Curious, Quaint Eccentric And Extraordinary In All Ages And Nations, In Art, Nature, And Science Including Many Wonders Of The-World.

Mackay, A. (1847) The Western World Travels In The United States In 1846-1847.

Mayhew, H. (1861) London Labour and London Poor Vol III.

McConnell Stott, A. (2009) The Pantomime Life of Joseph Grimaldi.

McMillian, S. (2012) Cooke's: Britain's Greatest Circus Dynasty.

Paterson, P. (1861) Glimpses of Real Life as Seen in the Theatrical World.

Percy, S. and Percy, R. (1826) The Percy Anecdotes, Original and Select Volume XII.

Preston, J. (1819) The Picture of Yarmouth: Being A Compendious History and Description of all the Public Establishments within that Borough.

Rendall, M. (2014) Astley's Circus: The Story of an English Hussar.

Sharp, J. W. (1847) The Vauxhall Comic Song-Book.

Stephens, J. L. (1845) Incidents of travel in Central America Vol II.

Stephens, J. L. (1848) Incidents of travel in Yucatan Vol II.

Tredennick, B. (ed) (2011) Victorian Transformations: Genre, Nationalism and Desire in Nineteenth Century Literature.

Turner, J. (2000) Victorian Arena: The Performers, A Dictionary of British Circus Biography Vol II.

Wallett, W. F. (1884) The Public Life of W. F. Wallett, the Queen's Jester: An Autobiography of Forty Years Professional Experience & Travels in the United Kingdom, The United States of America (including California), Canada, South America, Mexico and the West Indies.

Index

51162773R00101

Made in the USA
Charleston, SC
16 January 2016